NECKLACE
AND PENDA

NECKLACES AND PENDANTS

Angie Boothroyd

A & C Black • London

Every effort has been made to ensure that all the information in this book is accurate. However, due to differing conditions, tools and individual skills, the publisher and the author cannot be held responsible for any injury, losses or other damages that may result from the use of information in this book. Neither the author nor the publisher can accept any legal liability for any errors or omissions. All safety information and advice contained in this book should be fully adhered to. Jewellery-making can involve the use of dangerous substances and sharp tools. Always follow the manufacturer's instructions, and store chemicals (clearly labelled) and tools well out of the reach of children.

I am extremely grateful to all the artists who have contributed their images to this book, and most particularly to those who have shared their knowledge and expertise by allowing me to use step-by-step instructions for making selected pieces. Obviously, these are included in this book as practice exercises, so that you can learn new techniques, skills and effects by following an experienced teacher, and hopefully use your newly honed skills to work on your own designs and original ideas. Please respect the experience, generosity and copyright of the makers featured by using the designs and instructions included in this book in the spirit of learning; you should never attempt to pass off someone else's original design as your own.

FRONTISPIECE *Interlocking Spiral Necklace by Daniela Dobesova. Sterling silver, 22 carat yellow gold, 2005. Photography by Stuart Holt.*
TITLE PAGE *'Harlequin' Necklace by Angie Boothroyd. 18 carat green gold, 22 carat yellow gold, 22 carat red gold, tourmalines, 2006. Photography by Keith Leighton.*

First published in Great Britain in 2007
A & C Black Publishers Limited
38 Soho Square
London W1D 3HB
www.acblack.com

ISBN: 978-0-7136-7933-5

Copyright © 2007 Angie Boothroyd

CIP Catalogue records for this book are available from the British Library and the US Library of Congress.

Angie Boothroyd has asserted her right under the Copyright, Design and Patents Act 1988 to be identified as the author of this work.

Typeset in FB Californian

Book design by Susan McIntyre
Cover design by Sutchinda Thompson
Commissioning Editor: Susan Kelly
Copyeditor: Julian Beecroft

Printed and bound in China

This book is produced using paper that is made from wood grown in managed, sustainable forests. It is natural, renewable and recyclable. The logging and manufacturing processes conform to the environmental regulations of the country of origin.

Contents

ACKNOWLEDGEMENTS

This book is the product of the efforts of many people to whom I am greatly indebted. First and foremost I would like to thank all the chapter contributors who kindly donated their time to this project: Gabriella Balogh, Stephen Bottomley, Sigurd Bronger, Sonia Cheadle, Sarah Keay, Kirsti Reinsborg Grov, and Yen. This book could not have been written without their helpfulness and generosity. Many thanks also to the overwhelming number of people who took the time to send in images and suggestions for step-by-step demonstrations; the many offers that went unused are nonetheless much appreciated. Thanks also to those who helped in the dissemination of information during the planning stages: Tony and Christine at Dazzle, and the helpful people at ACJ and SNAG. Finally, thanks to Janice Hosegood and everyone at Electrum Gallery for letting me run riot there for an afternoon, to Amanda Doughty for quietly enduring many a headache-tinged meeting at Cockpit, and of course to Susan Kelly at A&C Black for instigating this book and for her steadfast support and encouragement over the last year.

Petal necklace by Angie Boothroyd. Fine and sterling silver, 18 carat green gold, 22 carat yellow gold, 22 carat red gold, 2005. Photography by Keith Leighton.

Introduction

WHO IS THIS BOOK FOR?

This is a practical book ideal for anyone wishing to broaden their jewellery-making skills, whether a practising designer/maker or a keen student. The sheer breadth and individuality of the demonstrations means that even seasoned professionals will find something new, while beginners will also be able to follow the projects as they are explained in detail.

If you are new to jewellery-making, you will benefit from the Basic Techniques appendix at the back, which outlines the fundamental processes used throughout the book and in jewellery-making on the whole.

WHY NECKLACES AND PENDANTS?

Neckpieces make great showpieces, their potential scale and drama unmatched by other forms of jewellery. This, and the lack of technical restraints involved, makes them the perfect medium for demonstrating a wide variety of methodologies.

Through step-by-step demonstrations and detailed photographs, the following chapters provide a glimpse into the working methods of several studio jewellers, each with their own distinctive approach. They have generously illustrated their techniques in depth, with the aim of sharing practical knowledge and providing inspiration.

HOW TO USE THIS BOOK

In each step-by-step chapter, a contemporary designer/maker demonstrates the making of a necklace or pendant of their own design, with particular emphasis on techniques which are unique or unusual. This information is shared by the makers in good faith, on the assumption that you will undertake the projects as a way of gaining new skills which can then be integrated into your own practice.

At the beginning of each chapter is a list of tools and materials required. While major or specialist equipment is included in these lists, it is assumed that you have some basic workshop tools (files, pliers, and so on); these are not generally listed, so as to avoid repetition. Most of the materials required will be familiar to the practising maker and readily available from bullion dealers. There are some notable exceptions, however (Japanese lacquer, for example), and extra care has been taken to provide sources for these more obscure materials in the supplier list.

Please note, it is crucial that you read the important health and safety notes where given, and that you do not proceed with any process if you are at all unsure about the necessary safety precautions.

If you are a beginner you may encounter some unfamiliar terms and techniques. To fill these gaps in knowledge you will find a Basic Techniques appendix, which is also useful for those who just need a quick refresher. The Glossary should also go some way to clarifying certain terms.

Finally, you are strongly advised to read a chapter in its entirety before embarking on a project, not only to make sure you have the necessary tools, but also to ensure you have a grasp on the project as a whole so that each step can be understood in context. You will find that many of the projects lend themselves easily to variation, so do feel free to experiment. An inquisitive attitude to making will multiply the possibilities arising from the following chapters.

OPPOSITE *Necklace by Tone Vigeland. Silver, 1992. West Norway Museum of Decorative Art, Bergen, Norway. Photography by Guri Dahl. This sculptural neckpiece is made up of countless handmade silver elements attached to a flexible silver mesh, creating a sensuous and wonderfully tactile piece. The artist's sophisticated use of repetition as an aesthetic device lends itself perfectly to dramatic pieces of jewellery, and she has since gone on to apply her methods to sculpture. Note how the lack of clasp here allows the work to flow without visual or structural interruption.*

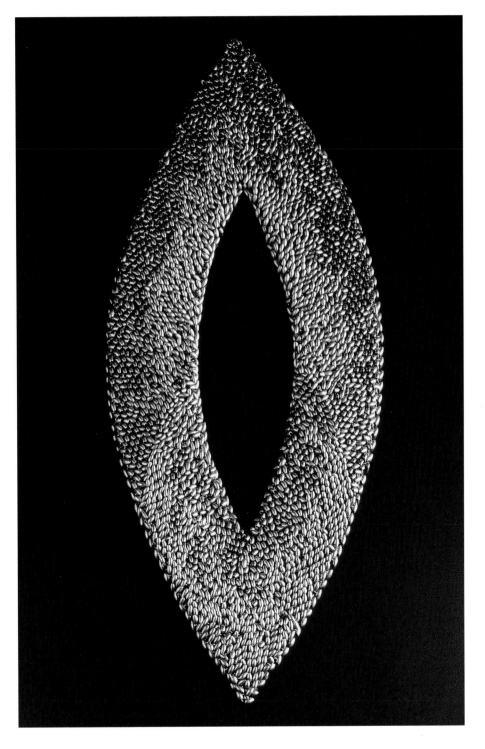

'Fragments of Ornament', necklace by Marianne Anderson. Oxidised silver (forged), 18-carat gold, garnets, pearls, 2005. Photography by Marianne Anderson. Inspired by the history of ornament, Marianne's fascination with traditional forms is evident in this piece, which is undeniably contemporary, yet resonant with historical decorative motifs.

1. Necklace Design

Although this book concerns itself with technique rather than design, it must be said that to overlook the design process is a perilous route to jewellery-making. For this reason it is worth mentioning here certain design issues which have particular relevance to necklaces and pendants.

Design needn't involve intricate hand-painted illustrations or computer-aided technical drawings. At its most elementary but critical level, good design is about taking into account how a piece is intended to be used – in the case of a neckpiece, how it will be worn: by whom, with what, on what occasion, where and why. Taking a moment to reflect on these questions of use will highlight more practical issues including the following:

NECKLACE OR PENDANT

Simply put, a necklace is a piece of jewellery which hangs from the neck. Whether a chain-like structure, a string of beads, or a work of art which uses the body as its platform, the term 'necklace' refers to the piece in its entirety. The word 'pendant', however, refers to a hanging object and not to the cord or chain from which it is suspended. (Technically, a pendant does not necessarily have to be hung from the neck; it could hang from a hoop earring, for example.) Although the semantics are unimportant (in reality, the terms are often misused), the difference between the two does have implications for the designer.

A necklace, especially a shorter one, tends to have close contact with its wearer. It often lies directly against the skin where, if it is a fluid form, it adapts to the shape of the neck and collarbone. There is no limit to what shape a necklace may take or how it interacts with the body; for this reason, necklaces of grand proportions (more often referred to as 'neckpieces') are often used as an ultimate form of creative expression.

A pendant (especially on a long cord) differs from a necklace in that it tends to have more separation from the face and body, functioning more as a stand-alone object, a statement, a small sculpture to wear. It is itself a focal point, the cord or chain usually being secondary. Because the conventional pendant does not meld with the body to the same degree as a necklace, the artist has complete liberty to explore three-dimensional forms with the freedom of a sculptor.

SCALE

The length of a necklace is not only a question of personal preference but of practicality. Shorter necklaces, up to about 18 inches (46cm), work equally well with collared shirts or low necklines, whereas longer styles are especially versatile as they hang forgivingly over most clothes. Bear in mind that a longer necklace will generally take longer to make, and will use more materials – potentially, a significant expense.

CLASP/ATTACHMENT TO BODY

Although a long necklace which fits easily over the head does not need a clasp, a shorter necklace will require some sort of closing system. A clasp needn't be viewed as an annoying contrivance; on the contrary, it can act as the focal point of a necklace, or at the very least a chance to complement the overall design of a piece. One chapter of this book is dedicated solely to the making of clasps, though a wide variety is also available ready-made from suppliers.

COMFORT

Because necklaces sit against the delicate skin around the neck, comfort is key. Sharp corners should generally be avoided, and new designs should be tested for discomfort, not to mention other unpredictable side effects. (I recall one well-known jeweller's story about a necklace she'd made partly of rubber – she wore it to a party only to find that she smelled of burnt tyres by the end of the evening.)

MATERIALS

Necklaces are by their very nature fairly large pieces, making them particularly expensive to make if gold or platinum are used (less so in the case of silver). As you will see in the following pages, however, non-precious materials – whether metals, textiles, or found objects – can be transformed into neckpieces that are very precious indeed.

If you do use precious materials, be aware that hallmarking law varies between countries, and changes often. (As I write, current hallmarking legislation is being challenged in the UK.) For this reason it would be worth your while to obtain the latest guidelines from your nearest assay office. (See the suppliers' list for details.)

2. 'Amass': Fused Wire Necklace
by Yen

INTRODUCTION

It is reassuring to discover that even the most dazzling structures can reveal themselves to be surprisingly uncomplicated. This sumptuous silver necklace by Yen is one such example. Its appearance is that of a complex linking system, impossibly difficult to construct; yet the reality is very different.

Only a few basic workshop tools are needed to make this piece; however, you will also require a healthy dose of good, old-fashioned patience due to the sheer number of miniscule elements which need to be made and assembled. Many makers enjoy this repetitive approach, and you may find it works well for you; repetitive processes such as this are often described as having a therapeutic effect – although for some the result is exactly the opposite!

One time-saving feature of this piece, though, is the use of manufactured chain. A great deal of contemporary handmade jewellery takes advantage of such factory-made products, and with good reason; if the chain in this piece were to be made by hand it would more than double the total making time.

TOOLS AND MATERIALS

Tools
- Soldering equipment (torch, soldering blocks, pickle)
- Basic workshop tools

Materials
- 0.7mm diameter (21-gauge B&S) sterling silver wire (for fusing)
- Sterling silver trace chain
- 1.2mm diameter (17-gauge B&S) 18-carat gold pin wire, white or yellow
- Clasp of your choice

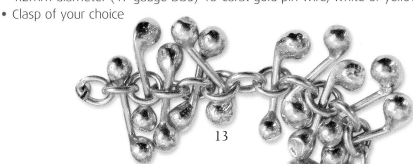

13

METHOD

1. Create fused wire ends

Use end cutters to snip off several equal lengths of wire, about an inch long. Taking one at a time, hold the wire vertically with the tweezers and direct the flame just below the lower end of the wire. When a ball begins to form, hold the flame directly on the ball and follow it with the flame as it moves up the wire. This should only take a few seconds.

> **TIP** You may need to flux the end of the wire to help it fuse. Use the hottest part of the flame, about a quarter of an inch beyond the central blue cone.

2. Secure the wires to the chain

Take a length of trace chain or similar (belcher chain would work equally well), thread the wires through the chain loops and then fuse the other ends. The wires will now be secured and unable to drop out of the chain loops. Don't thread a wire through every single loop, though; leave about every fifth one free.

Yen makes two versions of her *Amass* necklace – one in silver, and one gold-plated. With the latter, the plating is done at this stage, after the wires have been secured through the chain. The assembly is sent out to a plating service; it is rare for jewellers to do their own plating due to the toxic nature of the chemicals involved.

3. *Thread onto the core*

Use the empty chain loops to thread the chain onto the core wire. For the silver version, Yen uses 18-carat white-gold pin wire as the core; this is much stronger than silver wire but, being a white metal, has a similar colour to silver. For the gold-plated version, the core used is 18-carat yellow-gold pin wire; again, hardness and colour match are the deciding factors in the choice of wire.

TIP Pin wire, as its name suggests, is used primarily for making brooch pins. It is, however, extremely useful in many other jewellery applications. Unlike normal gold wire, pin wire is a special alloy which does not anneal when heated, so it is ideal for situations where a solder join is needed but where softening of the wire is not desired. It is readily available in 9-carat or 18-carat gold, and can be purchased in a coil or as a straight rod. Once you make pin wire your friend, you will wonder how you ever lived without it!

TIP Plating should be approached with care. On the gold version of this necklace, Yen plates the fused wire and chain, but not the core wire. This is because the core receives so much friction during wear that any plating would wear off quickly. It makes much more sense to use solid gold wire as the core; that way, no amount of wear will erode the colour. Unsurprisingly, 18-carat gold wire is naturally more expensive than silver, but if this means the necklace will maintain its appearance for longer, it is money well spent.

Solder a clasp onto the core wire (taking care not to heat the gold-plated chain and wire elements, if applicable). Finally, pickle the entire piece and apply a high shine using a barrel polisher. Pictured is the final piece in silver.

TIP Barrel-polishing is an efficient way of achieving a high shine and is especially useful on intricate objects such as this one, where using a polishing motor would be not only messy and time-consuming, but extremely dangerous. When choosing a barrel-polishing machine, make sure you buy one with a hexagonal drum, designed to polish metal; these are far more powerful than the cheaper, stone-tumbling variety.

Yen lives and works in London. Examples of her work can be seen on www.yenjewellery.com *Step-by-step photography by Angie Boothroyd. Final piece photographed by Rob Popper at Electronic Marketsquares.*

ABOVE *Group of four 'cluster' pendants by Catherine Hills. Silver, oxidised silver, 22 ct yellow-gold plate, 2000. Photography by Sue Baker.*

RIGHT *Nine-Pod 'cluster' pendant by Catherine Hills. Photography by Norman Hollands.*

Catherine's jewellery incorporates richly textured repeat units cast from masters of metal, wax or found objects. The bobbled surfaces are created on metal masters by making tiny metal granules (in a similar way to Yen's fusing of wire ends) and soldering them onto the surface. The entire form is then cast in multiples which are linked together.

'91 Triangles' neckpiece by Jane Adam. Aluminium, silver, stainless steel, 2003. Photography by Joël Degen. The universal appeal of the repeat unit is particularly effective when used in conjunction with large-scale kinetic structures such as this one. The artist first assembled 91 triangles of anodised, dyed and milled aluminium onto stainless steel wires, then suspended these from a silver and stainless steel neckband. Draped onto the body, the piece truly comes to life.

3. Knitted Wire and Felt Bead Necklace *by* Sarah Keay

INTRODUCTION

Imagine making a piece of jewellery only to find your hands are actually cleaner at the end of the process! If you yearn to escape the usual filth of the workshop and gain an insight into the wide world of textile techniques, then this project is the perfect introduction.

Techniques such as weaving and knitting have been used in jewellery for thousands of years, and have enjoyed a renaissance among studio jewellers in recent decades. Aside from the unique aesthetic qualities invoked by such methods, their popularity is largely due to their accessibility. This piece, for example, is relatively easy to make and requires only a few tools and materials. There is no soldering involved, and no chemicals – only washing-up liquid.

Here Sarah Keay shows you the basic process of knitting a tubular necklace out of wire, using a bobbin and a crochet hook. You will also see how to make felted 'beads' which can then be inserted into the knitted tube. Bear in mind that you can achieve wildly different results depending on your choice of bobbin, wire and wool. And because it can be constructed just as easily out of precious or non-precious wire, you have the choice of being as thrifty or as extravagant as you like. There is plenty of room for experimentation.

TOOLS AND MATERIALS

Tools
- Wooden bobbin (either 4-, 6- or 8-pegged)
- Crochet hook
- Scissors or wire cutters
- Round-nose pliers

Materials
- Reel of 0.3 – 0.5 diameter (29- to 24-guage B&S) wire (metal of your choice)
- Wool (for making felted beads)
- Washing-up liquid

METHOD

1. *Make the felt beads*

Start off by gathering a palm-sized clump of wool. Dip it into warm soapy water and, starting very gently, roll the ball between the palms of your hands. Continue dipping the wool into the water to keep it warm, and make sure there is enough soap to create a lather. Keep on rubbing the wool until it has felted – bonded together – and feels fairly solid. Allow to dry overnight.

TIP Washing-up liquid is normally used for felting, but if you have delicate hands, use baby bath instead.

TIP Don't take that worn-out jumper to the charity shop; if it's wool you can use it as felting material. Just unravel it a bit first.

2. *Wind the wire on*

Holding the bobbin firmly, with the thumb in front, push the end of the wire down through the centre of the bobbin, leaving about three inches spare. Wind the wire anticlockwise around one of the pegs. Then move on clockwise to the next peg along, and wrap the wire anticlockwise around it. Continue in this way until each peg has a loop around it. Be sure not to pull the wire too tight when knitting this first round, or you won't be able to pull the wire off the pegs in the next step.

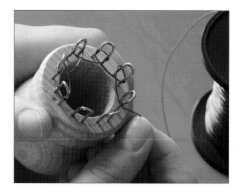

TIP Because there is no soldering involved in this process you can use any kind of wire you like, from the precious to the industrial.

3. Start the second row

Once you have wound the wire around all of the pegs, it is time to start the second row. Wind the next loop around the first peg, just above the existing loop, so there are two loops around the one peg.

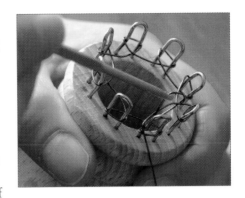

Using a crochet hook, take the bottom loop (the very first one you made) and lift it up and over the new loop, and off the peg completely.

Continue onto the next peg, making a loop and then pulling the bottom loop over it and off the bobbin. That's it – carry on in this way and soon a knitted tube will emerge.

4. Insert the felt beads

Every few inches or so, drop a felt bead into the tube and carry on. Keep knitting and dropping the beads in until your necklace reaches the desired length.

> **TIP** You could also use chunky plastic or glass beads in place of the felt, so long as they are not too heavy.

5. Cast off and join the ends

To finish the necklace, unhook all the loops from the bobbin. Cut the wire from the reel using scissors or wire cutters, depending on the hardness of the metal, leaving several inches at the end to work with. Loop this extra wire once through the last loop to prevent it unravelling.

To join the ends, continue to loop the wire through each opposite loop until the ends are completely joined. Use the round-nose pliers where your fingers won't reach. Snip the end off and tuck in towards the middle of the tube so it doesn't scratch.

6. *Pull to shape*
Gently pull the necklace into shape by crushing the wire in between the beads with your fingers.

Your knitted neckpiece is now ready to wear, and will have a graceful natural twist.

Sarah Keay lives and works in Dundee and can be contacted on sarahisobelkeay@hotmail.com
Step-by-step photography by K. Koppe.

Flower pendant by Hannah Louise Lamb. Oxidised silver, cerise silk, 2006. Photography by Hannah Lamb. A striking example of the integration of textiles into a piece of jewellery, the red silk used here adds a warm layer of colour and texture to an otherwise cool and hard-edged object.

'Knitted Necklace' by Giovanni Corvaja. Gold, 1998. Photography by Giovanni Corvaja. The subtle variations in colour in this knitted necklace were achieved by joining together 26 rods of different colours of gold and then drawing them down into wire. Because the colour difference between adjacent golds is so slight, the appearance is that of a smooth gradation from white to deep yellow.

4. Multicoloured Gold Necklace
by Angie Boothroyd

INTRODUCTION

What colour do you associate with 18-carat gold? The first image that springs to mind is probably the yellowish colour found in most 18-carat gold sold in the West today. This familiar hue, however, is not the natural colour of gold in its pure state (which is actually a much deeper yellow), but the result of alloying it with other metals.

By making your own gold alloys, rather than buying them as manufactured sheet and wire, you can have complete control not only over the colour and carat of your golds, but over other working properties such as hardness and ductility.

I tend to keep my necklace designs fairly simple so that the subtle differences in my gold alloys have a chance to shine. In this project I will show you the straightforward method I use to alloy golds, followed by step-by-step instructions as to how to make this *Palm* necklace.

In constructing the elements that make up this piece you will learn a few shortcuts I have developed over the years – including how to work harden, texture and shape the delicate components in one easy step. I will also provide useful tips regarding equipment, as well as hallmarking law – always a consideration when working in precious metals.

If you prefer, this piece can also be made in silver, ordinary manufactured gold sheet, or a combination of the two. Just skip the alloying process and proceed using the sheet material(s) of your choice.

TOOLS AND MATERIALS _____

Tools for alloying

- Scales (accurate to at least .1 gram)
- Scorifier and scorifier holder
- Ingot mould
- Soldering sheet
- Rolling mill
- Dark-lensed safety goggles (must be suitable for high-temperature work)
- Oxy-propane torch (or other high-temperature torch system)

Other equipment

- Disc cutter
- Basic workshop tools
- Plastic strainer
- Ultrasonic tank

Materials

- Fine gold casting grain
- Pure copper casting grain
- 18 ct jump rings, made of 0.5 mm thick wire and with a 2 mm inner diameter
- Fine silver casting grain
- 18 ct hard solder

HEALTH AND SAFETY NOTES!

The alloying described in this chapter requires the use of a high-temperature torch system. Seek professional advice when setting up such a system, as health-and-safety regulations vary. The company that sells you the torch should be able to advise you.

Always wear dark-lensed safety goggles when melting gold.

ABOUT GOLD ALLOYS

Gold in its pure form is too soft to be used in most jewellery, so it is commonly alloyed with other metals (usually silver and copper) to make it harder and more durable. The proportion of gold in any given alloy is expressed in terms of carats (not to be confused with the carat measure of gemstone weight, which is a different system altogether). Thus 24-carat gold is pure gold, also called 'fine gold'; 18-carat means that 18 out of 24 parts are gold – in other words, 18/24ths, or 75%; 14-carat gold is 14/24ths gold, and so on. This is why such a huge price difference exists between, say, 9-carat and 18-carat gold: a necklace in 9-carat gold would have only half the gold content of an identical piece in 18-carat.

While gold content is generally referred to in terms of carats in the United Kingdom and the United States, in Continental Europe it is customary to find it expressed as parts per 1000.

Three ingots

For example, 18-carat gold would be referred to as '750 gold' (750/1000 = 75%).

It is worth noting that even metals in their purest form (fine gold, fine silver, etc.) are not usually referred to as being 100% or 1000 parts pure. This is to account for the fact that trace levels of impurities are always present in even the most refined metals. Gold may be sold, for example, as 99.9% or '999'.

The working properties of any given alloy will vary depending on the elements used, and their respective proportions. For example, a typical 18-carat yellow-gold alloy contains roughly equal proportions of silver and copper. Raise the proportion of silver and the alloy becomes a greenish-gold colour ('green gold') and much softer. If a higher proportion of copper is added, a redder and harder gold is produced ('rose gold' or 'red gold').

GOLD CARATAGE CONVERSION TABLE

Carat	Percentage gold
24	99.99%
22	91.67%
18	75%
14	58.33%
9	37.5%

METHOD

1. *Make the gold alloys*

The gold alloys I use are made up of three ingredients: fine gold, fine silver and pure copper. You can buy all of these in casting-grain form, but you can also use scraps of wire, sheet and the like, so long as they are pure.

I make relatively small batches of gold at a time, using about 10 grams of fine gold per ingot. Obviously this makes sense in terms of cash flow, but it also has the advantage of limiting potential damage or loss resulting from mistakes.

After much experimentation I have found three alloys which are relatively easy to make and which have pleasing working properties – most notably, they are not particularly susceptible to cracking when rolling out; nor do they demand rigorous conditions or special precautions to alloy successfully. These are 18-carat green, 22-carat yellow, and 22-carat red gold. Their recipes are as follows:

Alloy	% Gold	% Silver	% Copper
18-carat green	75	21.4	3.6
22-carat yellow	91.7	6	2.3
22-carat red	91.7	0.8	7.5

Before you begin, make sure your bench is protected from heat with a large soldering sheet (a board made of asbestos substitute), and that the area is free from flammables.

Weigh out the required amount of each element, adding a bit of additional fine gold to be sure the gold content meets the minimum hallmarking requirements.

> **TIP** It is crucial that the gold content of each alloy weighs at least the designated percentage. While it is perfectly acceptable for your 18-carat alloy to have a gold content above 75%, if it falls even a hair below this percentage it will not pass the assay test and will therefore be 'unhallmarkable'. In the UK this means it is not legally allowed to be sold as 18-carat gold.

Cover the inside surfaces of the ingot mould with soot to ensure easy removal of the gold ingot. You can do this using a candle, or a propane flame without any air or oxygen added. In either case, hold the mould at a 45° angle above the flame and it will soon be blackened.

Put all three metals into a scorifier secured in a long-handled holder. Sprinkle with powdered borax. Here I used gold and copper in grain form, while the fine silver is scrap sheet.

> **TIP** You should have a separate scorifier for each alloy of gold to avoid cross-contamination. Write the name or carat of the alloy in pencil on the side of the scorifier.

Adjust the width of the ingot mould (I set mine to about 12mm) and clamp securely. Place on the soldering sheet.

Put on the dark-lensed safety goggles, light the torch, and heat up the ingot mould so it is just too hot to touch. This will prevent the molten metal from splattering out upon contact.

Heat the contents of the scorifier. Keep the flame moving to ensure the metals all receive the required heat.

When the metal starts to melt, tilt the scorifier slightly so the molten metal gathers in one place. Once it has reached the stage where a molten ball has formed, temporarily lay the scorifier down on the soldering sheet in order to free your hand. Grab a pinch of borax powder and sprinkle it onto the molten mixture. Pick up the handle again, gently swill the molten metal around to ensure it is free-flowing, and then carefully tip the contents into the ingot mould, keeping the flame on the molten metal as it is poured.

TIP Do a few dry runs first. Practice the action of picking up the scorifier holder one-handed and pouring the (imaginary) contents into the ingot mould until the motion becomes second nature. Only then should you attempt an actual alloy.

TIP Fine gold melts at 1064°C (1948°F) which is beyond the capability of an ordinary propane or mains gas torch. In the UK an oxy-propane torch system is often used for high-temperature work; in the United States an acetylene torch is common. Ask your equipment supplier for advice, as there are several options on the market, and important health-and-safety issues to be aware of.

The gold will set instantly. Unclamp the mould (carefully, as it will be hot) and inside should be a gold ingot like the one pictured.

> **TIP** If your gold ingot is not all in one piece, or has very long pour lines at the top, you may be pouring it in too slowly. This may take a while to master. But remember, it doesn't hurt to melt the gold repeatedly, so don't be afraid to do so until you achieve a nice, solid ingot.

Pickle each ingot to remove the borax. Then use the rolling mill to roll each one out into sheet. This is best achieved with several gentle passes through the mill rather than by a few forceful ones. You will also need to anneal several times along the way.

After each anneal, roll the metal in one direction only, as a change of direction without annealing will create conflicting stresses, causing the sheet to buckle. If you want to change direction, anneal the sheet first to relieve the stresses, and then change.

Use a dixieme gauge to keep an eye on the thickness of the sheet, and stop when it reaches about 0.5mm (.020 in.).

> **TIP** Silver can be alloyed in the same way as gold. To make sterling silver, cast an ingot of 92.5% fine silver and 7.5% pure copper.

2. Cut out and texture the components

Using a disc cutter, stamp out several discs of each colour gold (green, yellow and red); you don't need to use a disc cutter, but it is much quicker than piercing with a saw.

Fold a strip of emery or other textured paper in half. Arrange the discs along the paper in a staggered line; this will help prevent the strip from turning sharply to the left or right when put through the mill. It is important that each disc passes through the rollers alone; if several go through simultaneously the pressure will be distributed among them, causing unnecessary distortion.

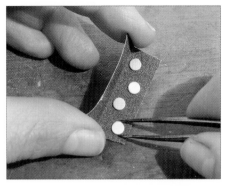

Adjust the rolling mill so you feel some resistance when putting the discs through. Do a few test pieces first, adjusting the rollers so the discs emerge at about twice their original length. With a single pass through the rolling mill you will simultaneously a) impress the emery texture onto the discs, b) stretch the discs into ovals, and c) work-harden the metal.

If the emery paper is stuck to the ovals, soak them in water for about five minutes to loosen. Then put them into a plastic strainer (not a metal one that will scratch) and rinse under a tap, using your hands or a sponge to remove the stubborn bits. Don't worry if a few little black specks from the emery remain; they will come off later in the ultrasonic. Dry.

3. *Clean up the edges*

File the edges of the ovals with a 4-cut flat needle file. Gently deburr.

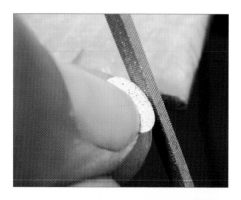

Take a pair of flat-nose pliers and wrap masking tape around each side. Holding the oval with the pliers, use a steel burnisher to burnish the edges. Usually about three passes with the burnisher will do: once dead centre, then once tilting very slightly left, and once slightly right, to ensure that the entire edge is burnished. Press as hard as you can without causing the metal to fold under pressure. (If it does, don't worry; it will be remedied a few steps later when the oval is folded in half.) The edges should now have a high shine, free of file marks.

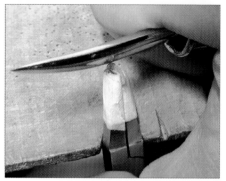

TIP Instead of using ordinary flat-nose pliers wrapped in masking tape, you could use pliers with nylon jaws, which will hold the metal securely without scratching.

One third of the ovals will need two holes in them – one at either end – and the remaining two thirds will need one hole only. How you divide up the different colours of gold is up to you.

Use dividers to mark an indentation 1 mm from the end(s) and drill using a 0.9mm ($^3/_{32}$ in.) drill bit. Deburr both sides of the hole using a round or stone-setting burr. (Just hold the burr in your hand and twist manually.)

4. *Fold*

Remove the masking tape from your flat-nose pliers. Place an oval between the jaws so that it is visually cut in half lengthways. If you drilled the hole(s) centrally you can use them as a guide.

Tap the oval over the edge of the pliers with a rawhide mallet until the gold is resting flatly on the pliers and a perfect 90-degree angle is formed.

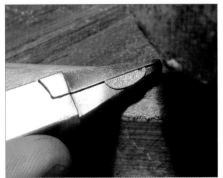

The finished components should look something like this. Now you are ready to assemble the 'leaves'.

5. *Assemble and finish*

Take one jump ring and thread four 'leaves' onto it. (Refer to the photo of the final necklace to see how they are arranged.) Continue assembling in this way until all the components have been used or the desired length is reached. When you are satisfied with the assembly, using the smallest possible flame solder each jump ring with a pallion (tiny piece) of 18-carat hard gold solder, taking care not to anneal the 'leaves'.

Add a clasp of your choice. When all the soldering is complete, pickle the piece, rinse, and place in an ultrasonic tank for at least ten minutes. This will remove any stubborn bits of emery impressed into the metal during rolling.

TIP Many jewellers use a microweld kit when they need a fine flame, but you can also adapt an oxy-propane torch head to do the same thing. I soldered a fine microweld torch tip into the middle of this gas arc head and then closed all the surrounding holes with silver sheet, soldered on with silver solder. It may not be the neatest looking job in the world but this torch head has helped me to solder several thousand jump rings over the years!

Finally, polish using a brass brush, a little water and plenty of washing-up liquid.

Rinse thoroughly, pat dry, and wear!

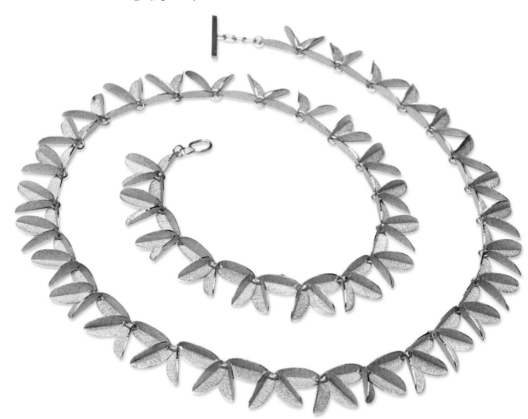

Step-by-step photography by Angie Boothroyd. Final piece photographed by Keith Leighton.

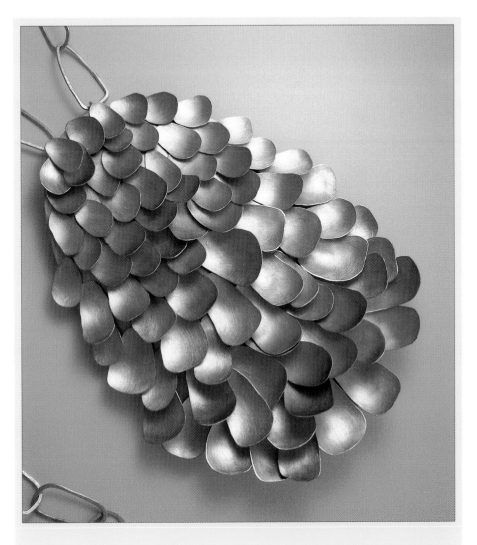

'Scale' pendant by Kate Bajic. Silver, 2003. Photography by Kate Bajic. Here silver sheet was pierced, drilled, filed, formed, forged and burnished to produce a collection of delicate elements which were then loosely attached to a base, allowing them freedom to move. There is a certain sensation of opulence in this collection of small, shimmering pieces of metal. The white finish is actually a thin layer of fine silver achieved by annealing and pickling the piece several times.

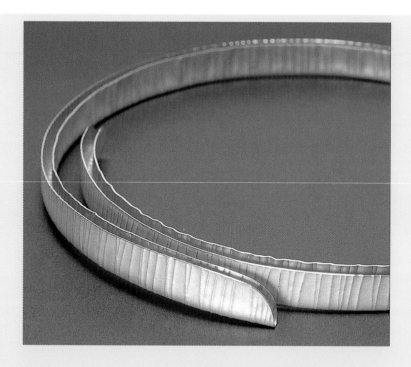

'Fold', neckpiece by Irene Metaxatos. 999 silver, 24 gold-plate interior, 2005. Photography by Irene Metaxatos. Inventive use of the rolling mill can generate all sorts of surface effects. The lined texture in this neckpiece was created by rolling the silver through the mill with several wires. The sheet was then folded by hand and formed into a circle on a mandrel. The depth of the pattern is especially evident in the wavy edge, where it becomes not just surface pattern but an integral part of the form. Its corrugated texture also adds structural stability.

5. Enamelled *'Molecule'* Pendant *by* Kirsti Reinsborg Grov

INTRODUCTION

Because a pendant hangs on the body in a very free and unrestricted way, it allows you the freedom to be as three-dimensional and sculptural as you like in your design. This *'molecule'* pendant by Kirsti Reinsborg Grov is a striking example of the impact that can be achieved by using what are essentially traditional working methods to create a playful piece of sculpture to wear.

The simple shapes and bold colours in this piece belie the meticulous craftsmanship behind it. Here you will learn exactly how it was created, from the construction of the spheres through to the meticulous enamelling process.

To achieve a beautifully smooth enamelled surface requires time and discipline, but if you follow the instructions and don't take any short cuts, you too can learn to incorporate the vibrancy of enamel in your work. There is also an element of surprise in this piece; one of the spheres is in fact a plastic ball from a children's atomic modelling kit. Consequently, this chapter will also explore the use of found objects.

TOOLS AND MATERIALS

Tools and equipment

- Doming block and punch
- Fibreglass brush
- Enamelling kiln
- Steel tongs
- Steel wire mesh
- Mortar and pestle
- Carborundum stone
- Film canister or similar container
- Distilled water
- Paper towels
- Basic workshop tools

Materials

- 0.5mm (.020 in.) copper sheet
- Vitreous enamel, opaque (powdered or lump form)
- Silver enamelling solder
- 'Atomic' ball and connector stick
- Elastic cord for neck

HEALTH AND SAFETY NOTES!

1. This chapter demonstrates the 'wet packing' method of enamelling, which is safer than using enamels dry as they are harmful if inhaled. Always apply enamels wet, and wear a mask when handling dry enamel.
2. Fibreglass breaks off into tiny splinters as it is used; keep yourself protected at all times when using the fibreglass brush. Wear protective gloves, safety goggles and a mask. Always brush under a running tap to ensure fibres are washed away, as they are harmful if inhaled.

If you are unsure about any health and safety aspects of this chapter then do not proceed without appropriate assistance.

AT A GLANCE: ENAMELLING

1. Grind and clean the enamel.
2. Clean and degrease the metal.
3. Apply wet enamel to the metal surface.*
4. Fire in the kiln and allow it to cool slowly.
5. Stone the surface.
6. Repeat steps 3–5 until a smooth surface is achieved. (Do not stone surface after final firing.)

*Some enamels benefit from a base layer of flux. Not to be confused with soldering flux, enamelling flux is applied in the same way as the enamels themselves. It is recommended you experiment with different flux/enamel combinations to see which results suit you.

METHOD

1. Construct the spheres

The arrangement of spheres in this piece requires careful planning. Read this section carefully and sketch out a design before starting.

To make a sphere, start by scribing two circles of equal size onto the copper sheet. Pierce out and anneal. Using a doming block and punch, form the discs into half-spheres, annealing as necessary along the way.

Before soldering together, either one or both discs will need a round hole pierced out wherever they are to be joined with other spheres. (In the example shown, Kirsti has cut holes in both halves, as this particular sphere will have adjoining spheres on both sides.)

Secure the two domes together with iron binding wire. Solder the seam with silver enamelling solder. (This solder is known by various names, but the important thing is that it has a very high melting point – higher than that of enamel, and will be used throughout this piece.)

Make several spheres in this way. However, note that in addition to the junction holes you will also need to include two smaller holes (about 4 mm in diameter) in the piece to allow the elastic cord to pass through. These can be on one sphere or two different ones, and should be pierced out after doming. To give them a neat edge, make two gold jump rings and solder them into these smaller holes with silver enamelling solder so that the copper edges are neatly covered.

There is one more thing to bear in mind: Kirsti's piece has a removable plastic ball from an atomic modelling kit added to it as the very last step. To accommodate this, one of the metal spheres needs to have an inverted dome soldered into it with a hole in the middle (look closely at the top-right photo on page 42). A plastic connector stick will be inserted here and used to connect the 'atomic' ball to the piece.

After soldering, remove the binding wire from the spheres and pickle for several minutes to be sure that all oxidisation is removed.

2. *Prepare the enamel*

Before use, enamel must be cleaned and ground to a fine powder. Both of these tasks are achieved using a mortar and pestle. Even if you are using enamel supplied in powder form do not omit this crucial step, as even the tiniest speck of dirt can ruin an otherwise flawless surface.

Put about a teaspoon of enamel into the mortar and fill halfway with tap water. Use the pestle to gently grind the enamel in a circular motion. Bear in mind that lump enamel will take some time to pulverise, while powdered enamel will require less effort. Then swill and pour the water down a sink, allowing the enamel to settle at the bottom of the mortar while the water carries away dust and

other impurities. Add more water and repeat the process, continuing to do so until the water runs clear. For the final rinse, use distilled water.

Now that the enamel is clean, care must be taken to keep it that way. Decant the wet enamel into a small container with a lid, such as a thoroughly cleaned film canister. Keep the lid on whenever the enamel is not being used.

3. *Counter-enamel the interior*

Because enamel expands and contracts at a different rate to metal, it is susceptible to cracking during the cooling process after firing. To prevent this, a counter-enamel is often used; in other words, enamel is applied to the back of the piece as well as to the front. So Kirsti enamels the inside of the spheres before soldering them to each other.

Surfaces to be enamelled must be clean and grease-free. Use a fibreglass brush to clean the insides of the spheres. Then apply the wet enamel to the insides of the spheres with a flat dental tool or similar implement. Be sure to cover the inner surfaces in their entirety.

After applying the wet enamel, soak up any excess water by carefully touching the torn edge of a paper towel to the edge of the enamel surface. Rest the spheres on a piece of steel wire mesh and, using steel tongs, place inside a kiln preheated to 800°C (1470°F). Once the surface of the enamel has melted to the point where it is smooth and glossy, it is fired and ready to remove.

This usually takes a few minutes but will depend on the firing temperature of the enamel and the temperature of your kiln. (It's best to do a test piece first and to check periodically.) Use the tongs to remove the mesh with the work on it, and place on top of the kiln to allow it to cool gradually; this helps avoid cracking.

TIP You can also use a plastic drinking straw to make an applicator tool; just snip off the end at an angle to make a fountain-pen shape.

TIP When choosing a kiln, bear in mind it is useful to have a window in the door so that you can check the progress of your firing without opening the door and letting heat escape.

4. *Solder the spheres to each other*
Take two spheres and file their joining holes flat with a flat file, providing maximum surface area for soldering. Secure the spheres together with binding wire. Solder with silver enamelling solder. Remove the binding wire and pickle.

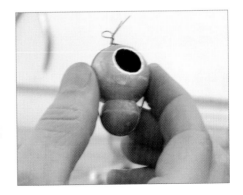

Repeat the filing, soldering and pickling process until all spheres are soldered into a 'molecular' structure. Clean with emery paper.

> **TIP** Normally you would do all the soldering first (with enamelling solder) and then do the enamelling. However, in this piece Kirsti chooses to enamel the sphere interiors before soldering them to each other. Heating a previously enamelled surface to soldering temperature can adversely affect the enamel's appearance, but in this case, because the counter-enamel is hidden, its appearance is unimportant.

As you can see here, Kirsti has soldered a small inverted dome into one of the spheres, with a small hole in the middle of it. This concave surface will support the plastic ball she will add as the last step.

5. *Enamel the exterior*
Clean the metal with a fibreglass brush under a running tap in preparation for enamelling.

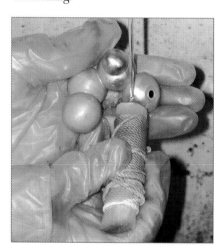

Apply the enamel to the exterior surfaces using the same technique as on the insides. Remember to draw off excess water with a paper towel. Fire as before, checking periodically on your progress.

After firing, use a carborundum stone and water to clean the enamelled surface and to key it in preparation for the next coat.

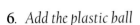

Apply a second layer of enamel and fire again. The number of layers required will vary, but in general several thin layers are better than a few thick ones. Anywhere between three and six layers is typical, with two as the absolute minimum. (Only one was used inside, but only because it is not visible. Several layers are needed for a really smooth surface.) Stoning is required after the application of each layer – though not after the final firing, after which the enamel should be left smooth and glossy.

6. *Add the plastic ball*

If you followed the modelling-kit approach you will now be able to attach the plastic ball just as if you were building a molecular model, using a plastic connector stick from the kit, allowing the ball to sit in the inverted dome recess created for it.

String through a piece of elastic cord and you are finished.

> **TIP** If using several colours of enamel, start with the highest-firing colour and work your way down to those that fire at lower temperatures. This ensures the already-fired enamels are not 'burned' by subsequent firings.

Kirsti Reinsborg Grov lives and works in Oslo and can be contacted on kirgrov@frisurf.no
Photography by Sigurd Bronger.

Using found objects:
Egg necklace by Sigurd Bronger

Sigurd Bronger is known for his witty use of found objects. For him the object is the focal point of the work, with the rest of the piece serving mainly as a neat and unobtrusive support.

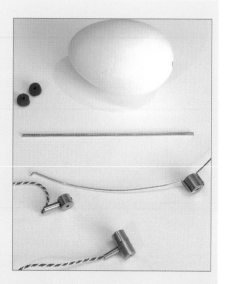

Using found objects requires ingenuity; you are always dealing with something new, and soldering an object into place is usually out of the question due to the heat required. Sigurd uses various cold connections – joins which don't require soldering, such as screws and tension fittings – to fix objects into place.

Parts prior to assembly.

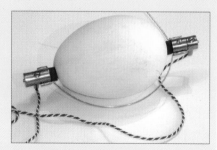

For this piece, a goose egg is hollowed out and a steel bar put through the middle. The end pieces, which are made from brass and are gold-plated, are placed at either end of the bar. Finally, a piece of steel wire is wrapped around and sprung into place, holding the entire assembly together.

Springing the wire into place.

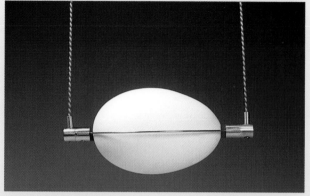

The finished necklace. Photography by Sigurd Bronger.

Multi-charm pendant by Jane Moore. Oxidised silver and enamel, 2006. Photography by John Moore. Anyone who has ever tried their hand at enamelling will know that really successful results are usually the product of hours of experimentation. Jane has developed her own unique approach to enamelling which involves using photo-etched silver inlaid with enamel and overlaid with enamel transfers which she designs and creates using Adobe Photoshop. The details of her technique remain a closely guarded secret, but this is nevertheless an intriguing example of what can be achieved with a persistent and investigative approach.

6. 'Euclid's Pendant': Photo-etched Pendant by Stephen Bottomley

INTRODUCTION

If you ever made sun prints as a child you will appreciate the magnificent detail that can be achieved by applying a mask to photosensitive paper and exposing it to daylight. In this chapter you will learn to apply similar principles to metal surfaces using the technique of photo-etching. This is a process that can be practised at home or in the workshop with a few specialist pieces of equipment, and the results can be strikingly precise.

Etching – the selective removal of metal by chemical means – is not a new process; however, photo-etching is a 20th-century development. The 'photo' in 'photo-etching' refers to the photographic process by which the design 'mask' is transferred to the metal before being immersed in the chemical etchant. Originally designed for use in the circuit-board industry, the technique has been embraced by artists of all kinds, especially jewellers and printmakers.

In this chapter Stephen Bottomley demonstrates through the creation of his *Euclid's Pendant* how photo-etching can be employed for both decoration and layout, especially when skilfully combined with traditional fabrication techniques.

TOOLS AND MATERIALS

Specialist photo-etching tools

- UV (ultraviolet) light box
- Photopolymer film
- Red safelight (for darkroom)
- 2 x plastic trays (for developing/ rinsing)
- Etching tank or plastic tray (for etchant)
- Ferric nitrate
- Sodium carbonate or soda crystals

Household tools

- Cardboard
- Masking tape
- Packaging tape
- Rubber gloves
- Household ammonia
- Scalpel or craft knife

Photo-etched Pendant

Workshop tools

- Rolling mill
- Basic workshop tools

Materials

- Sterling silver sheet, about 0.7mm (.028 in.) thick
- Two pieces of copper sheet, about 1mm (.040 in.) thick
- Silver for pendant bail
- Cord or chain for neck

HEALTH AND SAFETY NOTES!

Household ammonia

Household ammonia must be used with caution due to its strong vapours. Follow the advice on the bottle carefully and use in a well-ventilated room, or, preferably, outside. Dispose of ammonia responsibly or use a funnel to return it to its original bottle for future use.

Handling chemicals

Photo-etching involves the use of chemicals that can be dangerous if handled incorrectly. In this demonstration the chemical used is ferric nitrate, a salt etchant which is safer than the more commonly used, but hazardous, diluted nitric acid. Despite its relative safety, however, ferric nitrate should be handled with care, as should all chemicals. Always protect yourself by wearing rubber gloves, safety goggles, an apron and a respirator. Ask your local council about safe disposal of chemicals in your area, as regulations can vary.

Health-and-safety guidance should be supplied by your chemical supplier. If you are unsure as to any health-and-safety aspects of this chapter then do not proceed without appropriate assistance.

AT A GLANCE: PHOTO-ETCHING

The six stages of the photo-etching process are as follows:
1. Tooling: Making the photo tool
2. Preparation: Ensuring the metal is flat and grease-free
3. Lamination: Applying the photopolymer film to the metal
4. Exposure: Exposing the photopolymer film to UV light
5. Developing: Hardening the UV-exposed areas
6. Etching: Removing the metal from unexposed areas.

METHOD

1. *Tooling: Make the photo tool*

Stephen's pendant begins as a two-dimensional design, drawn on the computer in CorelDraw and printed directly onto clear acetate. The elliptical outlines will serve as guides for piercing, and the straight lines bisecting them will be guides for scoring. The pattern inside the ovals will be surface decoration. It does not matter whether you create your artwork digitally or by hand, so long

as it ends up as black-and-white artwork on acetate. (You may also draw directly onto acetate with a permanent marker or experiment with black ink for more spontaneous mark making.) Remember, it is the black areas of your design which will be etched.

TIP For a super-high-resolution photo tool, have your computer file output to a PMT (Photo Mechanical Transfer) by a digital-imaging company. If creating artwork digitally, you'll get the best resolution from drawing programs such as CorelDraw, Adobe Illustrator and Macromedia Freehand, as these generate vector artwork (as opposed to pixel artwork, as created by Adobe Photoshop) and can therefore print out at infinitely high resolutions.

---

2. *Preparation: Ensure the metal is flat and grease-free*

The silver sheet Stephen is using here already has a pattern on one side, which he applied using the etching transfer process described in the box below. The elliptical design will be applied to the untextured side of the silver.

ETCHING TRANSFER

You can transfer a photo-etched texture from one sheet of metal to another by putting both sheets through the rolling mill together, one on top of the other. The master sheet can then be reused several times over. For the master, use a metal that is harder than the sheet receiving the impression. Anneal the recipient sheet before rolling so that it takes the impression easily.

Anneal, pickle and quench the silver. Roll through the rolling mill to flatten, and continue by beating the metal completely flat with a rawhide mallet on a flat steel stake. You may need to anneal several times. (If the silver is really stubborn you can use a planishing hammer, but very carefully so as not to mark.)

Holding the metal at the edges, use a toothbrush, pumice and a little water to scrub until it is grease-free.

To test for degreasing, hold the metal under a tap; the water should run off in sheets with no beading. Once degreased, the silver must be handled only by the edges as the slightest fingerprint will contain enough grease to ruin your efforts. Wrap in a paper towel to keep clean.

3. *Lamination: Apply the photopolymer film to the metal*
Important! The photopolymer film is photosensitive and must not be exposed to bright daylight; it is best handled in a darkroom with a red safelight.

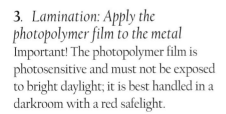

In the darkroom, cut a piece of photopolymer film slightly larger than the silver sheet. Upon close inspection you will see the blue photopolymer is actually sandwiched between two sheets of removable clear film and has a natural 'curl' to it. Remove the top protective sheet on the inside of the curl. (You will need to gently rub the corner of the sheet back to get it to separate.)

Carefully but firmly apply the photopolymer evenly to the silver, with the emulsion (blue) side facing the metal. Try not to trap any air between the metal and the film, as this can cause problems later on. Smooth out any large bubbles with your fingers, and cut away excess film from around the edges with a scalpel.

To ensure a good lamination you now need to put the silver through the rolling mill. But before you do this, you must protect the work from any daylight by placing it in a cardboard carrier (two pieces of cardboard hinged together at one end with masking tape). Hold the carrier firmly closed as you leave the darkroom.

As the work progresses through the rolling mill (taped end first) you will hear the crackling of tiny bubbles being squeezed out. After rolling, you may quickly inspect the sheet to ensure bubbles are removed – but only for a few seconds in indirect light. You might need two passes to de-bubble.

4. *Exposure: Expose the photopolymer film to UV light*

These instructions assume you are using a light box whose light shines from below; if yours has a light in the lid then everything will have to be flipped over. Place the photo tool (the acetate) in the UV light box. Lay the silver on top of it with the photopolymer facing down. (You will again be exposing the photopolymer to indirect daylight for a few seconds, so remember to keep this time to a minimum.) Close the light box as soon as possible.

Expose for between 5 and 30 seconds. (This will vary depending on your light box; refer to the manufacturer's instructions.) The UV light will pass through the clear areas of the photo tool and onto the blue photopolymer, thereby exposing it. The black areas of the photo tool will prevent light from reaching the blue photopolymer, leaving those areas unexposed.

> **TIP** Stephen uses an industrial printmakers' light box, but small home versions are available from electronics shops. See the suppliers' list for details.

When finished, put the silver back into the cardboard carrier and take it to the darkroom for developing.

5. Developing: Harden the UV-exposed areas

In the darkroom, prepare a plastic tray with a solution of 10 ml sodium carbonate to one litre of warm (20-22°C/68-72°F) water. If unavailable you can substitute sodium carbonate with ordinary household soda crystals. You will also need another tray of warm water for rinsing.

With only the red safelight on, take the silver out of the carrier and remove the remaining clear protective layer from the photopolymer film. (Do not forget this step! It is easy to overlook.)

Immerse the silver in the sodium-carbonate solution, rubbing gently and evenly with a soft cloth or cotton-wool ball. This process develops the exposed areas, while unexposed areas are dissolved away. The procedure should only take a moment, but it is important that you thoroughly remove all unexposed areas of photopolymer. Do not, however, leave the metal in the solution for longer than necessary, as over-immersion will dissolve all the photopolymer, whether exposed or not.

After development it is safe to turn the lights on. Rinse the silver in the warm water and use a sponge to gently remove all traces of developer. You should now see your design. Pat dry gently and leave to harden in daylight. The sheet will darken in colour slightly.

6. *Etching: Remove the metal from unexposed areas*

Use packaging tape to cover any metal you do not want etched – namely, the other side of the metal and all edges.

In order to etch the silver you will need a) the appropriate etchant (also called a 'mordant') for the particular metal being used, and b) a suitable etching container or tank. To etch silver, Stephen uses a 55% ferric-nitrate solution, which he puts in a heated bubble tank to ensure a clean, continuous etch. However, you can also use an ordinary plastic tray (see the 'tip' below for instructions).

TIP If you don't have access to a bubble tank you can use a plastic tray filled with warm etchant. Place the metal so the side to be etched is face down; this allows the metal to drop down away from the sheet as it disintegrates. Remove the sheet every half hour or so (wearing thick rubber gloves) and rinse to ensure thorough removal of metal. The etching process will be slower using this method due to the lack of constant heat, but it does work.

Wearing thick rubber gloves and appropriate eye protection, fill the tank with the 55% ferric-nitrate solution. Heat to about 35°C (95°F), but no more than 45°C (113°F). Carefully place the metal into the etchant. With the bubble tank, the etch will take between 45 minutes and 2 hours depending on the temperature of the etchant, so check the progress every half hour or so. When finished, remove the metal and rinse thoroughly. All exposed areas of silver (i.e. not protected by blue film or packaging tape) will now have been etched.

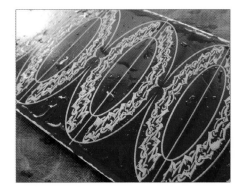

Remove the packaging tape. To remove the blue photopolymer, soak in household ammonia in a well-ventilated room. Rinse the metal sheet in water. You now have an etched piece of silver.

7. *Construct the pendant*

Using the etched outlines as a guide, pierce out the shapes with a saw. Guide the blade through the etched recesses, then file away until the etched lines are completely removed.

Stephen's design has alternating 'valley' and 'mountain' folds which have to be scored on alternating sides of the silver. The valley folds are scored along the photo-etched guidelines using a scriber and a straight-edge. They are then filed with a three-square needle file, followed by a square needle file. This opens the groove first to a 60°, then a 90° angle. (File just over three-quarters of the way through the metal with the three-square file before proceeding with the square one.) The resulting 90° groove will allow the metal to be folded at a 90° angle.

> **TIP** When scoring, file just deep enough that you start to see a faint line on the other side of the metal.

The mountain folds will be situated along the small tabs between the elliptical shapes. These need to be scored in the same way, but on the other side of the sheet. Other than the fact that they do not have the benefit of the photo-etched guidelines, they are prepared identically.

Once the scoring is complete, the piece can be folded with parallel pliers and by hand into its final shape. The join and all fold lines then need to be soldered with hard silver solder. Add a bail, smooth the edges of the piece with fine emery paper, and finish as desired. String onto a cord or chain and the pendant is complete.

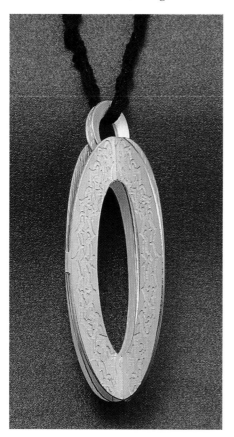

TIP Photo-etched recesses can be filled with vitreous enamel (using the champlevé technique) or even coloured resin. You could also oxidise the whole piece and then emery away the higher surface, leaving the etched areas dark.

TIP If you like the effect of photo-etching but not the mess, there is an alternative. There are companies that will do the photo-etching for you, either from your photo tool or from your digital file. See the suppliers' list for details.

Stephen Bottomley is the BA (Hons) Metalwork & Jewellery Course leader and senior lecturer at Sheffield Hallam University, and between 2005 and 2007 was chairman of the Association for Contemporary Jewellery, a UK-based membership network (www.acj.org.uk). More examples of his work can be seen on his website, www.seb-goldsmith.com

Many thanks to Sheffield Hallam University (www.shu.ac.uk/art) for allowing us to use their workshops for this chapter's demonstration.
Step-by-step photography by Angie Boothroyd. Finished pendant photo by Simone Nolden.

Photo-etching can also be used to cut components out of sheet without the need for piercing. This is accomplished by etching through the metal from both sides. (Attempting to etch all the way through from one side is not recommended for sheet over 0.5mm (.020 in.) thick, as the etch tends to get wider as it gets deeper.) The process is the same as for one-sided photo-etching but with the following changes:

1. Prepare two identical photo tools. They need to be larger than the metal being etched, and they also need identical registration marks – cross hairs or fine lines of some description – near the edges.
2. Apply the photopolymer film to both sides of the metal.
3. Place the photo tools one on top of the other so that the artwork lines up exactly. Hinge them together along one edge with masking tape.
4. Slip the metal in between the acetates and tape it into place, taking care not to obscure any metal to be exposed. Finally, tape the photo tools together all the way around at their edges, using the registration marks to check the alignment.
5. Expose one side of the metal, then the other.
6. Develop and etch both sides simultaneously.

Here Amanda created a photo tool for the front of the metal which had both a decorative pattern and a cutting line. The back photo tool had the cutting line only. When fully etched, the components dropped out of the sheet, patterned and ready for use.

'Roseflower' pendant by Amanda Coleman. Silver, cubic zirconia, 2005. Photography by Marcelo.

7. Japanese Lacquer (*Urushi*) Pendant
by Gabriella Balogh

INTRODUCTION

In this chapter you will learn the basics of *urushi* – an ancient Japanese lacquering technique rarely taught in the West. Practised in South-east Asia since ancient times, *urushi* requires great discipline and patience, but the results are very satisfying. The techniques shown here are in the Japanese style.

Urushi is in fact the sap, or lacquer, from the *urushi* tree. Botanically related to poison ivy, the sap is irritating to the skin; precautions must therefore be taken not to touch the *urushi* in its liquid form. During the hardening process, however, chemical changes take place which render the lacquer totally inert. Unlike other natural resins, hardened *urushi* also has the advantage of being resistant to water and acid, although it is susceptible to scratching so is best not worn next to other jewellery which may damage it. Care must also be taken to avoid prolonged exposure to UV rays which will cause fading, and for this reason a silk bag or a wooden box is often used for storage.

In the following pages, Gabriella Balogh generously shares the age-old techniques involved in the *urushi* process, using the same materials and methods that have been employed for centuries. As with all demonstrations in this book, you are advised to read through the chapter before commencing the project – you may be surprised at the length of time involved!

TOOLS AND MATERIALS

Specialist *urushi* tools and materials

- Small wooden spatula (for mixing the pigments and *urushi*, and for cleaning the brushes)
- Flat brush (for painting large areas of *urushi*)
- Thin cylinder brush (for painting thin lines and detailed areas)
- Bamboo tubes with silk filters, nos. 300 and 270
- Small metal spoon (for spooning the gold dust)

- *Sashime-urushi*
- *Kuronaka-urushi*
- *Kuroroiro-urushi*
- *Kijiro-urushi*
- *Nashiji-urushi*
- *Kijomi-urushi* (transparent yellowish) or *Nashiji-urushi* (transparent orange)

- Red pigment powder
- Yellow pigment powder
- Gold powder (*kin-pun*), grades no. 5 and no. 1
- *Tono-ko* powder (powdered burnt clay or pulverised whetstone)
- *Tsuno-ko* powder (deer-horn ashes)

Other tools and materials

- Wooden bead or similar base shape
- Cardboard box
- Spray bottle and water
- Piece of flat glass or ceramic tile
- Vegetable oil
- Thinner (turpentine or kerosene)
- Wet-or-dry emery paper,
  grades 400, 600, 800, 1500
- Piece of pure cotton fabric
- Silk cord for neck

HEALTH AND SAFETY NOTES!

Urushi in its liquid form is a skin irritant. Although many practitioners develop a resistance to its harmful effects, you are strongly advised to ensure the *urushi* does not come into contact with your skin.

METHOD

1. Prepare your Furo

Several coats of lacquer are required for this piece, with several days' drying time between each. While most resins require a dry atmosphere to cure, *urushi* is different. It actually needs to absorb moisture from the air in order to polymerise and therefore harden. You will need a small space with a relative humidity of 60%–80%, and a temperature above 20°C (68°F). The Japanese have a special humidifying cabinet for this purpose called a *furo*, meaning 'bath', which is typically made of wood, with sliding doors to keep humidity in and dust out. You can make a simple *furo*, however, out of a cardboard box. Just spray the inside of the box with water once a day to keep humidity levels up, and store in a warm room.

HANDLING OF TOOLS

The brushes and spatulas used to apply *urushi* need to be cleaned after each use to avoid hardening. Do this with a vegetable oil such as rapeseed oil. When cleaning the brushes, use a wooden spatula to work the oil through the hairs. Thoroughly remove the oil with thinner.

---

2. Choose a shape

Select a wooden shape for the pendant/bead. It should be free of knots, and therefore sap. If you are handy with wood you may wish to shape a piece to your own design.

Drill a hole so that you can thread your pendant onto a piece of cord when finished. It is important to do this now, as it is not a good idea to be drilling holes after the *urushi* is applied.

Make sure the wood is clean and dry. Abrade it with a piece of emery paper to remove any rough edges. Remove all traces of dust with thinner and a clean piece of cotton.

It is a good idea to find a long piece of wood or plastic such as a chopstick that fits firmly through the middle of the bead. This way you have something to hold on to while applying the *urushi* layers.

3. *Apply the foundation layers*

Using a flat brush apply a layer of *Sashime-urushi* to the bead. (This type of raw, very thick *urushi* is collected from the *urushi* tree at the end of the summer.) Put the piece in the *furo* and allow the lacquer to harden for four days.

Once hardened, abrade the surface with dry 400-grade emery paper. This keying of the surface ensures the next layer bonds correctly, thereby forming a strong, homogeneous structure – the key to *urushi*'s incredible strength. Clean the dust off with thinner.

Apply a second layer of *Sashime-urushi* in the same way and allow to harden in the *furo* for another four days. This time use wet 600-grade emery paper to abrade the surface. Remove dust with thinner.

For the third layer, use a 50/50 mixture of *Sashime-urushi* and *Kuronaka-urushi*.

Allow to harden for four days, then abrade with wet 600-grade emery and clean with thinner.

For the next two layers, use *Kuronaka-urushi*. After each layer, leave to harden for five days, and then abrade with wet 600-grade emery paper. Clean with thinner. For the final two foundation layers, use *Kuroroiro-urushi*. After each layer, allow five days' hardening and abrade with wet 800-grade emery paper. Clean with thinner.

Congratulations! You have now built up the *urushi* foundation. The next step is to make a decorative background.

> **TIP** Always clean dust and oil from surfaces with thinner before applying the next *urushi* layer.

AT A GLANCE: FOUNDATION LAYERS

Urushi type	Hardening time	Emery grade
1. *Sashime-urushi*	Four days	400 (dry)
2. *Sashime-urushi*	Four days	600 (wet)
3. Mixture of *Sashime-urushi* and *Kuronaka-urushi*	Four days	600 (wet)
4. *Kuronaka-urushi*	Five days	600 (wet)
5. *Kuronaka-urushi*	Five days	600 (wet)
6. *Kuroroiro-urushi*	Five days	800 (wet)
7. *Kuroroiro-urushi*	Five days	800 (wet)

4. Create the Nana-ko nuri background

Nana-ko nuri is a Japanese *urushi* technique whereby seeds or similar small elements are sprinkled onto the wet *urushi* surface, and later removed, to leave behind their impressions. In this instance the relief will then be filled with a contrasting colour *urushi*, after which the whole thing will be rubbed back to reveal a smooth, cell-like pattern.

Prepare a red *urushi* by mixing 12 parts red pigment powder to 10 parts *Kijiro-urushi* using a wooden spatula. Do this on a piece of glass or a flat ceramic tile. Save any leftover *urushi* by wrapping it in cling film.

Using the flat brush, cover the entire surface of the bead with red *urushi*. While the lacquer is still wet, use your fingers to sprinkle the plant seeds onto the surface. Then allow it to harden in the *furo* for three days.

Gently remove the seeds from the hard surface using a wooden spatula. Then leave to fully harden for another four days. You will be left with a 'cratered' surface.

60

Cover this surface with *Kuroroiro-urushi*, applied with the flat brush. Leave it to harden for six days.

Apply another layer of *Kuroroiro-urushi* and leave for another six days minimum. Make sure the *urushi* is completely dry in between these layers or it will come out when the surface is rubbed back in the next step. Repeat this layering process as many times as necessary to build the 'craters' up level with the raised areas – remembering to wait at least six days between each layer!

Once the recesses have been satisfactorily built up, use wet 800-grade emery paper, followed by 1500-grade, to rub the surface back until it is flat and the red 'crater' outlines just become visible. Clean with thinner.

Using a piece of pure cotton, polish the surface with a mixture of *Tono-ko* powder and vegetable oil until the surface is smooth and shiny. Then clean the surface with thinner.

AT A GLANCE: *NANA-KO NURI* BACKGROUND

1. Apply red *Kijiro-urushi*, sprinkle with seeds, leave for three days.
2. Remove seeds, harden for four days.
3. Apply *Kuroroiro-urushi*, harden for six days.
4. Repeat last step until surface is flush.
5. Emery smooth with 800- and 1500-grade emery paper.
6. Polish with a mixture of *Tono-ko* powder and vegetable oil.
7. Clean with thinner.

Now you are ready to apply the main motif.

5. *Create the Maki-e motif*

Maki-e, another technique unique to the Japanese lacquer tradition, involves the sprinkling of gold or silver dust onto the wet *urushi* surface. For this project you will first create another seeded texture then apply the *Maki-e* surface using two grades of gold powder.

Prepare a yellow *urushi* by mixing 10 parts yellow pigment powder to 10 parts *Kijiro-urushi*, using a wooden spatula.

Draw your design onto a piece of tracing paper. Turn over and trace your lines as accurately as possible on the back of the paper with the yellow *urushi*, using a thin cylinder brush.

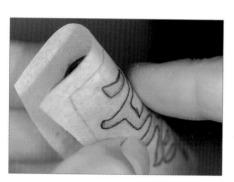

Press this wet *urushi* line onto the surface of the bead. Allow two days' hardening.

Then, using the hard outline as a guide, fill in your design with yellow lacquer, again using the thin cylinder brush. Be sure also to go over the original outline, as the entire area needs to be wet for the next step.

Sprinkle the plant seeds onto the wet surface. Allow three days' hardening.

Remove the seeds with a wooden spatula.

Wait three days. (Do not emery this surface back; this time we will be keeping the 'cratered' texture.)

Prepare the gold powder (*kin-pun*) as follows: Starting with grade no. 5 powder, carefully unfold the packet on a table, and weigh down the corners to secure it. (This is to be done in a strictly draught-free area!) Use a metal spoon to transfer a small amount of gold powder into the open end of the no. 270 bamboo tool.

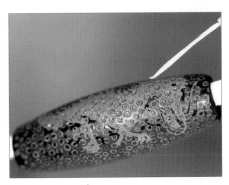

Keeping the gold-filled bamboo tool within reach, cover only the yellow motif (not the whole bead) with an extremely thin coat of *Kijomi-urushi* or *Nashiji-urushi*. Depending on the intricacy of your design you may use a thin cylinder brush or a flat brush.

With the surface still wet, apply the *kin-pun* by gently tapping the bamboo tool, allowing the gold to filter through the silk and onto the wet lacquer.

Use the dry flat brush to 'sweep' the gold from the surrounding dry areas onto the wet lacquer. Tap out any excess gold left in the brush back into the no. 5 gold packet.

Immediately repeat the sprinkling and sweeping process using a finer grade (no. 1) gold powder and a no. 300 bamboo tool. This time, tap the excess powder from the dry brush into a separate container or paper packet, as this will be a mixture of no. 5 and no. 1 and therefore should not be mixed into either original packet. Allow the lacquer to harden for five days.

Fix the gold dust by applying a layer of *Nashiji-urushi* with a flat brush and/or thin cylinder brush, whichever is the most suitable for your design. Allow another five days' hardening.

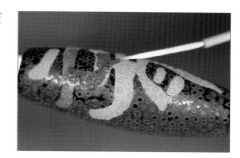

Polish the surface of the motif with a mixture of *Tono-ko* powder and vegetable oil using a wad of pure cotton. Clean the oil from the surface with thinner.

Cover the surface of the motif with extremely thin *Kijomi-urushi* or *Nashiji-urushi*, using clean cotton fabric. Leave for six days.

Polish with a mixture of *Tsuno-ko* powder and vegetable oil, using only the pad of your finger to rub it in. Clean with thinner.

Repeat the last two steps (applying the *Kijomi-urushi* or *Nashiji-urushi*, waiting and polishing) until the desired shine is achieved. You do not need to clean with thinner after the very last *Tsuno-ko* polishing.

AT A GLANCE: MAIN *MAKI-E* MOTIF

1. Transfer design onto pendant using yellow *urushi*. Leave for two days.
2. Fill design with yellow *urushi*.
3. Sprinkle plant seeds onto wet *urushi*. Leave for three days.
4. Remove seeds and leave for three days.
5. Paint *Kijiro-urushi* onto design and sprinkle with no. 5 and no. 1 gold powder. Leave for five days.
6. Paint on *Kijomi-* or *Nashiji-urushi* and leave for five days.
7. Polish with *Tono-ko* powder and oil. Clean with thinner.
8. Paint *Kijomi-urushi* onto main motif and leave for six days.
9. Finger-polish using *Tsuno-ko* powder and vegetable oil. Clean with thinner.

Repeat steps 8 and 9 until the desired shine is achieved. (No thinner is required after the very last *Tsuno-ko* polishing.)

Hang on a silk cord and wear!

Gabriella Balogh lives and works in Tokyo and Budapest. She can be contacted on gabriellaart@gmail.com. Examples of her work can be found on http://www.geocities.com/gabiurushi and http://www.japaneselacquer.artnet.hu.

Step-by-step photography by Gabriella Balogh. Final piece photographed by Angie Boothroyd.

'Navel' necklace by Sigurd Bronger. Hard foam, lacquer, steel, lenses, leather band, 1996. Photography by Sigurd Bronger. Challenging the intricacy of traditional decorative lacquer work, this contemporary interpretation is striking in its bold use of colour, allowing the form itself – not the surface – to take centre stage. The process is nevertheless painstaking: this piece was coated with no less than 20 layers of lacquer.

8. Clasps

The clasp can make or literally break an otherwise perfect piece of jewellery. There are as many approaches to clasps as there are to necklaces; this chapter illustrates several approaches, starting with a step-by-step demonstration for you to try. It is hoped these examples will inform and inspire you to develop your own unique approach to this important aspect of necklace design.

CLASP BY SONIA CHEADLE

Elegant clasp systems feature strongly in Sonia Cheadle's jewellery. The example demonstrated here is integral to the necklace itself. Because it works purely on tension, accuracy of gap widths and sheet thicknesses is critical.

Special tools
• Gap file 0.9mm (0.036 in.)

Materials
• 18 ct gold ball chain (length = length of necklace) x 12
• 2 cm (¾ in.) length of 18 ct gold rectangular tube, wall thickness 0.7mm (.028 in.)
• 2 cm (¾ in.) length of 18 ct gold round tube x 2
• 18 ct gold sheet, 0.9mm (.036 in.) thick

METHOD

Start with a length of rectangular tube. Because this shape is not readily available in gold, Sonia made a master in silver and had it cast in 18-carat gold. If you choose to cast the tube you will need to clean up the casting thoroughly before continuing; this means cutting off the sprue and going over all surfaces with an emery stick until smooth.

With a saw, pierce a groove down the middle of one of the thin sides of the rectangle, then clean up the gap using a 0.9 mm gap file. Solder a piece of sheet to one end of the tube to seal it shut.

> **TIP** Gap files have teeth on one edge only and are very useful when a groove of a specific width is required.

Drop the ball-chain ends into the groove until the tube is full. You may need to adjust the length of your tube at this stage so that the gap is just long enough to accommodate the ball chain without too much free play.

Now solder a piece of sheet onto the other end, thereby locking the chain permanently in place.

For the other half of the clasp you will need two equal lengths of gold tube and a narrow piece of 0.9mm (0.036 in.) thick gold sheet that is slightly longer than the tubes. Use a a 0.9mm (0.036 in.) gap file to make a gap along one length of tube.

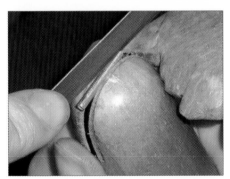

Slot the sheet into one of the tubes.

Now do the same with the other tube: file a gap and slot the sheet into it so that both tubes are now squeezing the sheet, with a thin strip of sheet exposed between them. This gap needs to be just under 1 mm in width (in other words, just wide enough to accommodate the thickness of the

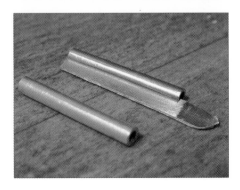

0.7 mm rectangular tube wall, allowing a bit extra for safety). Solder all the seams at once and cut the excess sheet from the ends.

Make another slot along the length of one of the tubes, directly opposite the slot that now contains the sheet. Cap off three of the four tube ends. Drop the chain ends into the open slot in the same way as before. Then cap off the last open tube end to secure the chain.

You have now finished constructing not only a clasp, but an entire necklace. Clean all clasp surfaces with emery and apply the desired finish. Sonia used a fine frosting wheel that creates a lustrous, semi-matte surface.

The clasp should start to slide into place quite easily and should feel tighter as it closes.

When fully closed, the clasp should feel tight and secure.

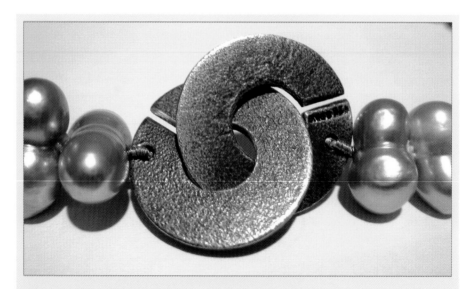

'C' clasp by Ghita Ring

This clasp is amazingly simple yet effective. It works on the puzzle principle; the two halves need to be twisted and turned a certain way in order to free them from each other – an arrangement they are not likely to fall into when hanging on the neck. Photography by Angie Boothroyd.

Button clasp by Tanvi Kant

For this piece Tanvi made a button out of porcelain and threaded it onto one end of the necklace. It then slips through the loop at the other end, simply and effectively completing the textile reference. Photography by Angie Boothroyd.

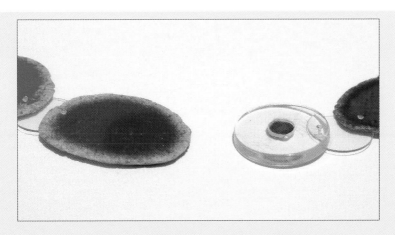

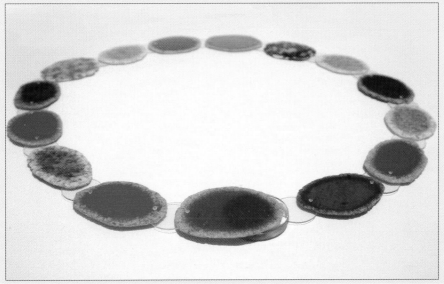

Magnetic clasp by Sarah Lindsay

This unobtrusive magnetic clasp is a neat solution for necklaces in almost any medium. Sarah embeds a small magnet in the centre of a clear plastic disc and glues a steel disc to the underside of the corresponding plastic component. When worn, the clasp is invisible. Photography by Angie Boothroyd.

> **TIP** Magnets are incredibly useful in jewellery, but best applied to pieces made of non-precious materials. Hallmarking laws (which vary from country to country) have a tendency to prevent the use of non-precious metals in otherwise precious pieces.

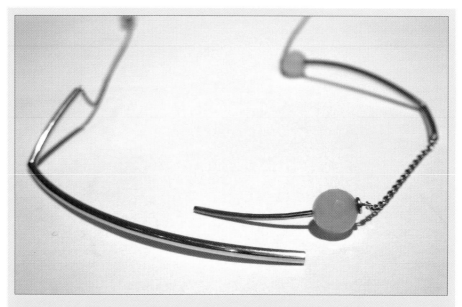

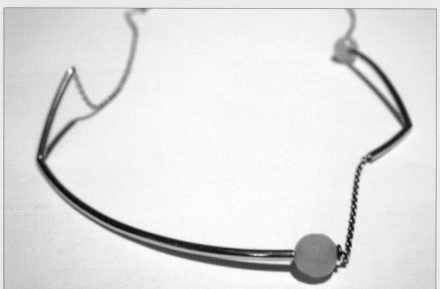

Tube clasp by Kamilla Ruberg

This invisible clasp consists of a curved piece of wire and a slightly less curved piece of tube. When the wire is pushed into the tube, the slight difference in curvature means the wire is effectively sprung into place. This principle lends itself to endless variations. Photography by Angie Boothroyd

Necklace with multiple clasp system by Lilian Busch

Necklace by Lilian Busch, Tahitian pearls, 9 ct gold, 2005. This inventive clasp system allows the necklace to be worn in endless combinations; two or three times around the neck, opera-length, or any way the wearer chooses. The light-coloured pearl row can also be wrapped twice around the wrist and worn as a bracelet with one of the 'rings'. Photography by Alistair Laidlaw.

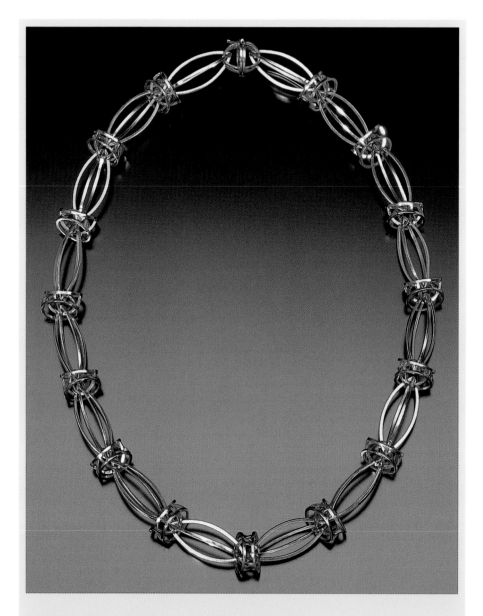

Necklace with integral clasp by Gina Pankowski

'Lattis Number 9' necklace by Gina Pankowski. 18 ct gold. The clasp in this piece is so well integrated into the overall design that it is barely visible at first glance. Gina designed this closing mechanism so that it could be cast, fabricated and customised to suit her many necklace designs. Photography by Doug Yaple.

Appendix: Basic Techniques

Whether you are a newcomer to jewellery or a practitioner who just needs a brush-up on the basics, this chapter should prove a useful reference. It outlines the most basic of techniques used by metals-based jewellers on a day-to-day basis; as such they are essential to many of the projects in this book.

PIERCING

Tools

- You will need a jeweller's saw frame and a saw blade. Saw blades are sold by the dozen in varying sizes from grade 4 (coarsest) to 6/0 (finest). 2/0 is a good, general-purpose size suitable for most jewellery work; 4/0 is another popular size for smaller jobs.

> **TIP** Adjustable saw frames are best, as they can be shortened to accommodate broken saw blades.

TECHNIQUE

Secure the blade into the frame so that the saw teeth are facing outwards (away from the body of the saw frame) and down. Secure the top end of the blade into the frame first. Then rest the top of the saw frame against your bench peg and push into the handle with your shoulder or sternum, compressing the frame slightly. With the frame flexed under pressure, secure the bottom end of the saw blade into place. Relax and allow the frame to return to its normal position, thereby pulling the blade taut. Pluck the blade with your finger to check for tightness; it should make a high 'ping' sound.

Place the metal flat on the bench peg with the area to be cut spanning across the V-shaped cut-out in the peg, or hanging off one edge. When you begin piercing, place your thumbnail directly next to the cut to prevent the blade from skidding across the metal. Start on an upstroke – this will make a tiny indentation – then get your thumb out of the way and continue sawing, cutting on the downstroke. Other than that initial upstroke, all cutting is done on the downstroke, so ease off when returning the blade to its upper position.

To pierce a straight line, tilt the saw forward so the blade runs at a 45-degree angle to the metal; this makes it difficult for the blade to twist off course. By the same token, to make a curved cut, hold the blade vertically to allow easy turning.

To pierce a hole in the middle of a piece of sheet, you need first to drill a small hole in the metal, then thread the saw blade through it. Secure the blade back into the frame under tension and pierce as normal.

FILING

Tools

- In terms of size, jewellers usually use three types of file: hand files (large), needle files (small) and escapement files (smallest). Hand files are about 6 in (15 cm) long and available in a variety of grades, referred to as 'cuts'. (Cut 2 is a good all-purpose grade to start with.) A glance at any jewellery supplier's catalogue will reveal the wide variety of shapes available. Needle files are much smaller, and available in similar cuts and shapes to their larger counterparts. Escapement files are minuscule and available only in fine cuts. It is worth noting that hand files are sold without handles; these need to be bought separately.

TECHNIQUE

The exact technique will depend on the job, but there are a few guidelines to follow.

Securely hold the object to be filed. This can be with your hand or with a tool such as a pair of pliers. It is best to rest the work directly on the bench peg; otherwise, rest the tool or your hand on the peg. Do not file in the air.

Choose a file which matches the shape of the object to be filed as closely as possible. For example, to file the inside of a curve, you would need a half-round or crossing file.

When filing the outside of a curve, use a flat file (or the flat edge of a file) and move it in a graceful arc – not in a series of flat strokes. Filing is done on the forward stroke, so apply pressure as you move the file forwards, and relax as you bring it back.

ANNEALING

Annealing is the process of softening metal through the application of heat. The metal will then remain soft until it is work-hardened.

Tools

- To anneal you will need a torch (there are many to choose from, so seek advice from a supplier) and a few soldering blocks; these are typically made of charcoal or asbestos substitute.

TECHNIQUE

Arrange the soldering blocks in such a way that they support the object while reflecting heat onto it. If the object is flat, it should not be placed flat on top of a block, but rested at an angle to allow the heat to flow freely around it. (This also ensures that any residual solder pallions from previous jobs do not melt onto the metal.) The colour of the metal when heated is used to judge temperature. Silver and gold are annealed when they reach a dark

cherry-red colour. Once this is achieved, remove the source of heat. Different metals require quenching at different stages of cooling, but most metals are best quenched after they have cooled to a black heat. To remove oxides formed during the heating process you will need to pickle the metal. (See 'Pickling' below.)

SOLDERING

Tools and materials

- To solder you need heat in the form of a torch. You will also need a flux of some kind to prevent the metal from oxidising and to facilitate the flow of solder. Borax is widely used as flux for silver and gold, as is Auflux. Finally, you need the appropriate solder for the metal you are joining. Silver solder and gold solder are both available in a range of melting points, referred to as hard, medium and easy, with 'hard' having the highest melting point. Enamelling solder has an even higher melting point than hard solder; because it is designed to withstand the high temperatures required for enamelling it can be used to join parts prior to firing in the kiln. For most jewellery work, the solder needs to be cut into pallions first using tin snips or end cutters.

TECHNIQUE

If you are using borax you will need to prepare it prior to soldering. Borax is sold as a solid cone and is used together with a borax dish. Put a few drops of water into the dish. Grind the bottom of the cone on the base of the dish, pressing firmly down to create friction. The borax will dissolve into the water to create a liquid solution which should resemble skimmed milk in colour and consistency.

Ensure the metal to be soldered is clean and free of grease. Use a small paintbrush to apply the flux to the join. Gently heat the area until the flux has bubbled up and reduced back down. Allow the metal to air-cool. Flux the solder pallions and place on the join, ensuring they touch both sides of the seam. Draw off any excess flux with a dry brush to avoid it swelling again and displacing the solder pallions. Finally, to solder, heat the entire piece, not just the join. (This applies especially to silver; with gold you may be able to just heat the area around the join.) Use a reducing flame whenever possible, and remove the heat the instant the solder has flowed into the join.

It is critical when soldering that all components reach soldering temperature at the same time. If one piece is hotter than the other, the solder will run onto it without bonding to the cooler component.

PICKLING

After annealing or soldering, metal will be dark with oxides and, where it has been used, hardened flux. The metal is cleaned by immersing it in a solution called a pickle.

Tools and materials

- A popular product to use is safety pickle, a powder which is simply dissolved in water. It is used to clean gold and silver as well as base metals such as copper, brass and gilding metal. It works best when warm and small amounts can be heated carefully in a glass jar over a tea light; however, professionals tend to use specially made pickle tanks or acid baths which are thermostatically controlled. Do not boil the pickle.

> ## HEALTH AND SAFETY NOTES!
>
> As with all chemicals, care must be taken not to get pickle in your eyes, and contact with the skin should also be avoided.

TECHNIQUE

Hot metal must be cooled before being immersed in the pickle; it can either be allowed to air-cool or it can be quenched – dipped in cold water. (This cooling process prevents dangerous splattering of the pickle and could save your eyes and your clothes.) To quench, use brass or copper tongs to pick up the metal and dip it into the water, then carefully place it in the pickle. On no account should steel or iron tongs be used, as ferrous metals will contaminate the pickle upon contact. If you are picking up a cool piece of metal, plastic tongs are suitable.

The strength and temperature of the pickle will affect its efficiency; a warm, freshly mixed pickle should remove flux and oxides in less than five minutes. Once the metal looks sufficiently clean, remove it with plastic, copper, or brass tongs, and rinse thoroughly to remove all traces of pickle.

Do not be surprised to see that your silver piece has acquired a white patina after pickling. This is a very thin layer of fine silver, the result of copper having been removed from the surface during pickling, and is easily removed.

MAKING AND CLOSING JUMP RINGS

Jump rings are best made in quantity; it is much easier and far more efficient to produce a whole batch than to construct them one at a time.

Tools and materials

- You will need three basic tools: a jeweller's saw, a pin vice, and a rod of silver steel with a hole drilled through it near one end. In the absence of steel rod, a wooden dowel can be substituted, although it will not be as durable. The diameter of the rod or dowel will determine the inner diameter of the jump rings. For the jump rings themselves, you need a length of round wire; the thickness is up to you. To close the jump rings you will need two pairs of flat or snipe-nose pliers.

TECHNIQUE: MAKING

Secure the undrilled end of the rod into the pin vice. Insert the wire into the drilled hole so it just sticks out the other side.

Hold the pin vice in your left hand (assuming you are right-handed) and twirl the vice clockwise to coil the wire around the rod. Make sure you hold the wire taut against the rod and against the coil itself so that no gaps appear. Make the coil as long as you like.

Release the coil from the rod by piercing or snipping it near the hole. Remove from the rod and hold the coil firmly between your left thumb and forefinger. Use the 'V' in your bench peg to help squeeze your fingers together. Using a piercing saw with a fine saw blade (a 6/0 blade to cut 0.5mm (24-gauge B&S) wire, for example), cut through the coil at an angle so that you are cutting through several rings at a time. (Be careful not to cut through to the back of the rings!) If you are lucky the jump rings will gather at the bottom of your saw blade, but usually they fall off so be sure you have something underneath in which to catch them.

TECHNIQUE: CLOSING

Using two pairs of pliers, open the jump ring not by pulling the ends outwards but by twisting them apart and simultaneously pushing them in, making the diameter of the jump ring temporarily smaller.

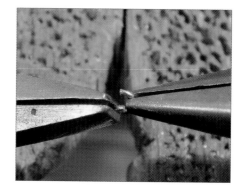

When you return the jump ring to its closed position, it will naturally want to spring shut and you will have to pull slightly to allow the ends to snap into place. This way, there will be no gap between the ends, which will be closed under tension.

DRILLING

Tools

• You will need a drill bit of the required diameter and a drill of some sort with which to drive it. There are several types of drill to choose from: Archimedes drills and bow drills are good low-tech options, but more commonly seen is a pendant motor with a flexible shaft (often referred to as a pendant drill). You also need a centre punch and hammer, and a drop of light machine oil to lubricate the drill bit.

TECHNIQUE

Secure the bit into the drill. On a firm surface, hold the centre punch on the metal and tap with a hammer to make an indentation. Dip the drill bit into the machine oil and proceed to drill into the dent, which will prevent the drill from skidding across the metal.

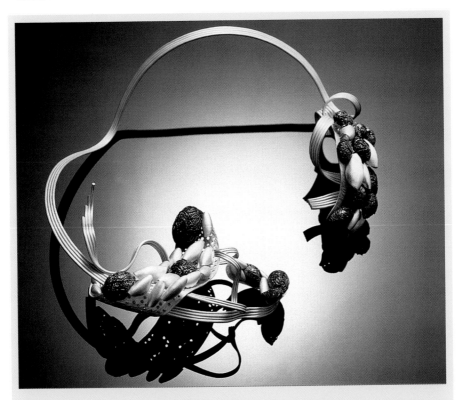

'Glowing I' neckpiece by So Young Park. Sterling silver, copper.

'Meminisse' necklace by Alison Macleod. Silver, smokey quartz, cherry quartz, amazonite, bra bits, found objects, ribbon, 2005. Photography by Shannon Tofts.

Appendix: Suppliers

Thanks to the Internet, geography is no longer a barrier to obtaining specialist equipment and materials. Several of the companies shown here sell their products online, and many operate a traditional mail-order service in addition to a retail shop. The section here on general suppliers of jewellery tools, materials and equipment is broken down by country, while the more specialised sections simply list suppliers alphabetically.

JEWELLERY TOOLS, MATERIALS AND EQUIPMENT

United Kingdom

J. Blundell & Sons
16 Hatton Wall
London EC1N 8JH
Telephone: (020) 7404 0744
Website: www.jblundell.co.uk

This well-established shop sells a range of bullion, tools and findings.

Cookson Precious Metals/Exchange Findings
Birmingham branch:
59–83 Vittoria Street
Birmingham B1 3NZ
(0845) 100 1122

London branch:
49 Hatton Garden
London EC1N 5HY
Telephone: (020) 7400 6500
Website: www.cooksongold.com

Billed as a 'one-stop shop' for all your jewellery-making needs, Cookson offers an impressive selection of tools, materials and equipment. A wide range of finished chains is included as well as pendant cords in silk, leather and rubber. Get a copy of their latest catalogue so you can order by phone and avoid the queues, or order your goods online.

Sutton Tools
Thomas Sutton (B'ham) Ltd
83 Vittoria Street
Birmingham B1 3NZ
Telephone: (0845) 094 1884
Website: www.suttontools.co.uk
Email: info@suttontools.co.uk

A comprehensive range of jewellery-making supplies and equipment is available from this long-established company based in Birmingham's famous jewellery quarter.

H.S. Walsh & Sons Ltd
Beckenham branch:
243 Beckenham Road
Beckenham
Kent BR3 4TS
Telephone: (020) 8778 7061

London branch:
44 Hatton Garden
London EC1N 8ER
Telephone: (020) 7242 3711

Birmingham branch:
1–2 Warstone Mews
Warstone Lane
Hockley
Birmingham B18 6JB
Telephone: (0121) 236 9346
Website: www.hswalsh.com

A comprehensive online shop now complements the three showrooms of this major supplier of tools and equipment for jewellers and watchmakers.

Wires.co.uk
18 Raven Road
South Woodford
London E18 1HW
Telephone: (020) 8505 0002
Website: www.wires.co.uk
Email: dan@wires.co.uk

This division of the Scientific Wire Company sells a range of wire in a variety of colours and materials, in small quantities suited to the craftsperson.

USA

Metalliferous
34 West 46th Street
New York, NY 10036
Telephone: +1 (212) 944 0909
Website: www.metalliferous.com

This Manhattan shop supplies silver and base metals as well as a range of tools.

Rio Grande
Telephone (toll-free from within the USA): (800) 545 6566
Telephone (from outside the USA): +1 515 839 3011
Website: www.riogrande.com

Rio Grande boasts three hefty catalogues: Tools & Equipment, Gems & Findings, and Display & Packaging. Each comprises several hundred full-colour pages, and simply browsing through them is an education in itself. You are unlikely to find a better range of supplies anywhere.

Belgium

Swiss Axe
Rijfstraat 11
B2018 Antwerpen
Telephone: +32 (0)3 232 10 90
Website: www.swissaxe.be
Email: info@swissaxe.be

This company sells tools and equipment for jewellers and watchmakers. Their website is written in English.

Briamhor
Vestingstraat 36
2018 Antwerpen
Telephone: +32 (0)3 231 31 76
Website: www.briamhor.be

Another good supplier of general tools, equipment and materials for jewellers and watchmakers.

Austria

Josef Felber
Siebensterngasse 30
A-1070 Wien
Telephone: +43 / 1 / 5232473
Email: kontakt@j-felber.at
Website: www.j-felber.at

This Vienna-based shop is a good source of general jewellery-making tools and equipment.

Ögussa
Postfach 1
Liesinger Flur-Gasse 4
A-1235 Wien
Telephone: +43 / 1 / 866 46-0
Email: office@oegussa.at
Website: www.oegussa.at

In addition to supplying metals for technical industries, Ögussa is a major supplier of precious metals to the jewellery trade. Their website can be viewed in several languages.

The Netherlands

Bijou Moderne
Edisonlaan 36-38
2665 JC Bleiswijk
Telephone: +31 (0)10-5296600
Email: info@bijoumoderne.nl
Website: www.bijoumoderne.nl

A popular supplier of tools, equipment and materials.

Germany

Burger Edelmetalle

Im Steinig 9
D-75210 Keltern-Weiler
Germany
Telephone: +49 (0)72 36 93 88 0
Email: info@burger-edelmetalle.de
Website: www.burger-edelmetalle.de

Burger is a supplier of bullion and findings and offers a good selection of precious metal alloys. Their website is written in English and German.

Karl Fischer GmbH

Berliner Strasse 18
Postfach 567
D-75105 Pforzheim
Telephone: +49 (0)72 31 31 0 31
Email: info@fischer-pforzheim.de
Website: www.fischer-pforzheim.de

A valuable resource for tools, equipment and findings, Fischer offers an extensive catalogue plus an online shop in English and German.

PHOTO-ETCHING SUPPLIES AND SERVICES

Chempix Ltd

Vantage Way
Birmingham B24 9GZ
Telephone: (0121) 380 0100
Email: paul.crutchley@precisionmicro.com
Website: www.chempix.com

A division of Precision Micro, Chempix is a small company offer an etching service aimed at jewellers and other small-scale makers. Metal can be etched from your artwork or digital file.

Sally Dyas

The Rocquette Villa
Rocquettes Lane
St Peter Port
Guernsey GY1 1XT
(01481) 711130
Email: s_dyas@hotmail.com

Sally sells Photec, a brand of photopolymer film, by mail order; she can supply relatively small quantities suitable for independent designer/makers.

Intaglio Printmaker

9 Playhouse Court
62 Southwark Bridge Road
London SE1 0AT
Telephone: (020) 7928 2633
Email: info@intaglioprintmaker.com
Website: www.intaglioprintmaker.com

This specialist retailer of printmaking materials and equipment is a good source of photo-etching supplies such as sodium carbonate.

Jessops

Website: www.jessops.com

This major retailer of photographic supplies is a useful source of darkroom equipment such as the red safelight required for photo-etching.

Maplin Electronics

Telephone: (0870) 429 6000
Email: customercare@maplin.co.uk
Website: www.maplin.co.uk

The small UV light exposure unit sold by this nationwide electronics specialist is an ideal size for small jewellery projects.

Rose Chemicals

Telephone: 020 7241 5100
Fax: 020 8809 7937
Email: sales@rose-chemicals.co.uk
Website: www.rose-chemicals.co.uk

Rose sell chemicals by mail order, including ferric nitrate.

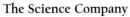

The Science Company
Telephone: (800) 372 6726
Website: www.sciencecompany.com

Makers in the US can purchase ferric-nitrate crystals online from this company.

ENAMELLING SUPPLIES

Diatherm – Vitrium Signum
Gresham Works
Mornington Road
North Chingford
Essex E4 7DR
Telephone: (020) 8524 9546
Email: diatherm@talk21.com

This is probably the most comprehensive supplier of enamelling supplies and equipment in the United Kingdom and run primarily as a mail-order service. They also supply photopolymer film for photo-etching. Phone for a catalogue.

WOOL

Wingham Wool Work
70 Main Street
Wentworth
Rotherham
South Yorkshire S62 7TN
Telephone: (01226) 742 926
Fax: (01226) 741 166
Email: wingwool@clara.net
Website: www.winghamwoolwork.co.uk

This mail-order house is the largest specialist supplier of fibres to felt-makers and textile artists in the United Kingdom. The shop is only open to the public two days a week, so check the opening hours on the website if you plan on calling in.

JAPANESE LACQUER (URUSHI) SUPPLIES

Tokyu Hands
12–18 Udagawacho
Shibuya-ku
Tokyo
Japan
Telephone: +81 (0)3 5489 5111
Website: www.tokyu-hands.co.jp (Japanese only)

This Japanese department store chain (full title: Tokyu Hands Creative Life Store) has branches throughout Japan and in Taiwan. Their website is in Japanese, but information about the chain in English can be found at en.wikipedia.org/wiki/Tokyu_Hands.

Watanabe-Syoten
6-5-8 Ueno
Taito-ku
Tokyo 110-0005
Japan
Telephone: +81 (0)3 3831 3706
Fax: +81 (0)3 3831-3500
Website: www1.odn.ne.jp/j-lacquer
Email: j-lac@par.odn.ne.jp

A specialist in Japanese lacquer tools and materials, Watanabe-Syoten caters to the every need of the urushi artist. Orders can be placed through their comprehensive website, which is written in Japanese and English.

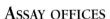

ASSAY OFFICES

London Assay Office
Telephone: (020) 7606 8971
Email: admin@londonassayoffice.co.uk
Website: www.thegoldsmiths.co.uk

Sheffield Assay Office
Telephone: (01142) 755 111
Email: carsona@assayoffice.co.uk
Website: www.assayoffice.co.uk

Birmingham Assay Office
Telephone: (0121) 236 6951
Email: michael.allchin@theassayoffice.co.uk
Website: www.theassayoffice.co.uk

Edinburgh Assay Office
Telephone: (0131) 556 1144
Email: swalter@assay-office.co.uk
Website: www.assayofficescotland.co.uk

In the United Kingdom, precious jewellery must carry a hallmark; this service is provided by the four assay offices listed above. Phone your nearest one for a registration pack.

A list of national authorised hallmarking offices designated under the Hallmarking Convention can be found at:
www.hallmarkingconvention.org/pages/ member/assay.html

Bibliography

BOOKS

Bowie, Hamish, *Jewellery Making* (London: David & Charles, 1976). ISBN 0-7153-7044-8

Edwards, Rod, *The Technique of Jewellery* (London: Batsford, 1977). ISBN 0-7134-0197-4

Malm Brundtland, Cecilie, *Tone Vigeland Jewellery + Sculpture Movements in Silver* (Stuttgart: Arnoldsche, 2003). ISBN 3-89790-185-4

McCreight, Tim, *The Complete Metalsmith* (Worcester, MA: Davis, 1991). ISBN 0-87192-240-1

McCreight, Tim, *Practical Joining* (Portland: Brynmorgen, 2006). ISBN 1-929565-16-X

McGrath, Jinks, *Basic Jewellery Techniques* (Edison, NJ: Chartwell, 1998). ISBN 1-55521-904-7

Richards, Alison, *Handmade Jewellery* (Oxford: Phaidon, 1976). ISBN 0-7148-1698-1

Untracht, Oppi, *Jewelry Concepts and Technology* (London: Robert Hale, 1982). ISBN 0-7091-9616-4

WEBSITES

www.wikipedia.org
www.urushi-kobo.com
www.chemicalelements.com
www.acj.org.uk
www.snagmetalsmith.org

Glossary of Terms

Acetate – Clear film available in sheet. Certain types can be printed on directly from a laser or inkjet printer.

Alloy – Any metal consisting of two or more elements.

Anneal – To soften metal by altering its microstructure through the application of heat.

Assay – To test a metal for fineness (caratage).

Auflux – A liquid soldering flux suitable for silver and gold.

B&S – Brown and Sharpe. Wire gauge commonly used in the USA, also known as AWG (American Wire Gauge).

Bail – Component attached to a pendant to allow it to be suspended from a cord.

Ball chain – Type of chain made of linked-up spheres.

Base metal – A non-precious metal such as copper, brass or nickel.

Belcher chain – Type of chain, similar to trace chain, made up of broad, interlinked loops of D-shape or similar wire.

Borax – A white powder sold as a solid cone for use as a flux in soldering. Also sold in powder form, useful for alloying. Also called sodium borate.

Bullion – Precious metal in large quantities, or as sold in the jewellery trade (sheet, wire, grain, etc.).

Carat – Relative content of gold in an alloy, expressed as parts out of 24. Also spelled karat. Not to be confused with the unit of measure for diamond weight, which is also spelled carat.

Clasp – The means of closing a necklace or other piece of jewellery.

Copper – Metallic element with the symbol Cu. Often used as part of gold alloys, and as a constituent of sterling silver.

Dividers – Tool similar to a drawing compass, used for scribing circles on metal or for marking set distances.

Dixieme gauge –Tool used to measure the thickness of metal.

Draw down – To decrease the diameter of wire by pulling through decreasing sizes of holes in a drawplate.

Etchant – See 'Mordant'.

Felt – Textile produced by bonding together of wool fibres.

Ferric nitrate – Chemical compound used as an etchant for silver. Also called iron nitrate.

Findings – Jewellery components such as clasps, jump rings and pendant bails.

Flux (soldering) – A substance applied to an area being soldered to improve the flow of solder and to prevent oxidisation. See 'Borax'.

Flux (enamelling) – Type of vitreous enamel often employed as a base coat prior to application of coloured enamels.

Gold – Metallic element with the symbol Au. It is a deep yellow colour and is the most malleable and ductile of all metals. It is typically alloyed with other metals to add hardness and strength.

Gold-plating – Process whereby a thin layer of gold is deposited chemically or electrochemically onto a metal surface.

Hallmarking – Stamping of a precious metal object as proof of having passed an assay test.

Ingot – Cast block of solid metal.

Ingot mould – Steel block into which molten metal is poured to make an ingot.

Jump ring – Loop of wire, typically used to link small components together.

Mordant – A liquid used to etch metal.

Opera length – Term used to describe the length of a pearl necklace as being 28–34 inches (71–86cm).

Oxy-propane – Type of torch system using a combination of propane and oxygen.

Precious metals – High-value metals such as gold, silver and platinum.

Reducing flame – A flame which removes oxygen from the atmosphere and therefore prevents oxidisation of the metal being heated. It is achieved by first establishing the flame using gas only, then introducing only enough air or oxygen (depending on the torch system) to eliminate the yellow end of the flame.

Rolling mill – Piece of equipment through which metal is rolled, primarily to stretch it and reduce its thickness. Many have both smooth rollers for sheet and grooved rollers for wire.

Silver – Metallic element with the symbol Ag. Typically alloyed with copper to create sterling silver. Also used as a constituent of gold alloys.

Solder – (n.) Metal used for joining other metals. It typically contains a high proportion of the metals being joined, plus added ingredients to reduce its melting point. When melted, it bonds to create a join. (v.) To join two or more pieces of metal together using solder.

Sterling silver – Alloy of 92.5% silver and typically 7.5% copper.

Trace chain – Simple style of chain made of interlinked round or oval loops.

Ultrasonic Tank – Device which uses high-frequency vibrations in a liquid bath to remove dirt and grease from metal.

Urushi – The common name given to the *rhus vernicifera* tree, or the lacquer derived from it. Also used to describe the decorative art of applying the lacquer to objects.

Vitreous enamel – Powdered glass which is fused to metal through firing.

Work-harden – To increase the mechanical strength of metal through deformation processes such as rolling, bending and forming.

Index